Covers for Sofas and Chairs

Soft Furnishing Workshops

Covers for Sofas and Chairs

Professional skills made easy

hamlyn

Contents

First published in Great Britain
in 2001 by
Hamlyn, an imprint of Octopus
Publishing Group Ltd
2–4 Heron Quays, London E14 4JP

Copyright © Octopus Publishing
Group Ltd 2001

Distributed in the United States
and Canada by
Sterling Publishing Co., Inc.
387 Park Avenue South,
New York, NY 10016-8810

ISBN 0 600 60232 X

A CIP catalogue record for this book
is available from the British Library

Printed and bound in China

The Publishers have made every
effort to ensure that all instructions
given in this book are accurate and
safe, but they cannot accept liability
for any resulting injury, damage or
loss to either person or property
whether direct or consequential
and howsoever arising.

This book first appeared as part of
The Hamlyn Book of Soft Furnishings

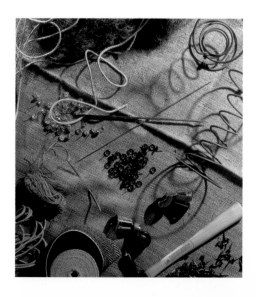

Metric and imperial measurements
Both metric and imperial measurements have been given in the instructions throughout this book. You should choose to work in either metric or imperial, but do not mix the measurements to ensure your projects' success.

Introduction

A WIDE RANGE of chairs, both upholstered and timber or metal framed, can be given a new lease of life with a decorative fabric cover. It might be that the furniture is sound but the seating fabric is past its best, or that you have moved to a new home and the decorations are creating problems with patterned textiles that no longer fit the bill or blend with their new surroundings. New, shaped loose covers or simple, straight-sided slip-over covers can be the answer; throws and rugs can become instant cover-ups, while old drop-in seats can be easily re-covered with new fabric.

Interior style

By looking at the home style magazines and manufacturer's brochures you can see how design schemes are put together in different styles of rooms. Fabrics and soft furnishings need to be chosen to suit the overall style, and the seating is often a major purchase within the scheme.

Experiment with tester paint pots and samples of wallpaper and furnishing fabrics until you find the design scheme to suit. By learning to mix and match colours, patterns, textures and accessories, and by following your own design instincts, you will soon create an attractive mix in your home.

If you are looking for a starting point for a decorating style to suit you, thinking about the particular interests and passions in your life might offer a theme around which you can work. If you love gardening, a floral theme or leafy green colours can set the style of a room. If you enjoy travel, you can have fun planning your room schemes around different countries. Think about developing a richly coloured Indian living room or a Mexican dining room. Alternatively, you can build a room scheme around a favourite collection – be it ornaments, old iron keys or musical instruments.

Making an inspiration board

Since there is so much choice when it comes to paints, wallpapers and good-quality, affordable soft furnishing fabrics, it can be hard to decide on a room's design scheme. To help you, try compiling an inspiration board made up of the images and items that appeal to you.

Tear out ideas from magazines and brochures – you will never find a whole project to suit you, but pick out the most pleasing aspects. Collect snippets of fabrics that attract you for their colour and design, paint swatches, flower colours – in short, anything you find pleasurable to look at.

Top *Market stalls or greengrocer's shelves piled high with flowers or fresh produce are rich sources for imaginative colour groupings for interior design.*

Above *The symmetry of stunning architectural details may inspire you with a previously unimagined decorating scheme for your home.*

Far left *Old sofas can be revived with loose covers, throws or rugs in patterns and styles that coordinate with your existing decorating scheme.*

The arrival of soft seating

Early furniture was made solely of wood. It was heavy, very solid in its construction and crudely carved. Towards the end of the 17th century, after years of people sitting on hard wooden chairs yet horse riding in comparative comfort, a craftsman came up with the idea of applying saddlery techniques to the seats of chairs. Thus the first upholstered chair was produced. The craft was very crude in its techniques at first, but upholstery methods were soon refined and perfected and, with the exception of springing, the methods have remained largely unchanged to this day.

Right *Making up your own inspiration board lets you discover the colours, styles and textures that you like. Build up the board gradually and be prepared to revise the look as necessary.*

After a few weeks of collecting different items for your inspiration board you will find a pattern emerging. You might find that texture dominates, or that two particular colours really stand out, or that architectural form is the strong point. From this selection you will know whether you prefer random prints, stylized prints or no print at all; and whether you prefer a cluttered country look or a chic minimalist style. You will soon be able to spot immediately anything that does not work and you will discover that colour tones and values are more important than precise colour matching. If your choices appear to be limited, do not worry:

a comfortable home revolves around very few colours. It is in fact the variety of texture and accessories that create a room's atmosphere and personal style.

Seating fabrics – practical considerations
Seating fabrics need to last, so choose carefully. Think about the practicality and suitability of furnishing materials before considering the final colour and pattern. For example, if you like pale fabrics on armchairs, but know that this would not be suitable for your home life, consider a second set of covers or throws to indulge your preference

Above *If you want to protect new chairs from small children or pets, fringed woollen rugs make ideal instant cover-ups and can be easily washed.*

Left *Soft and fluid to handle, chenille weaves are very popular and make excellent throws and cushions for sofas and armchairs.*

Fabric quality

The thread count of a fabric indicates how closely woven it is. The type of yarn used to weave the fabric also affects its durability. For upholstery and loose covers, ask for fabrics with a high rub test. This is a test that manufacturers use to find out how well a fabric wears. Sofa and chair covers, window seats and seat cushions need a minimum rub test result of 35,000 and preferably 50–60,000.

in the summer months, but give the seating a more practical finish during the winter, when everyone spends a lot more time indoors. Bear in mind the following points:

- Loose cover fabrics need to be heavy enough to withstand pets and boisterous family wear for many years, but be light enough to stitch with a normal sewing machine. They should be washable and not show every mark, and be colourful enough to be interesting.

- The piped edges of cushions and covers wear quickly, so check that the quality of fabric used is at least as good as the main fabric. You could use the same fabric or a contrasting colour from the same range.

Above *The simple lines of this sofa make it perfect for covering with semi-fitted loose covers when it becomes shabby or you want a different look. Equally, it can be covered up with a large bedspread or blanket, although this style of cover-up requires constant straightening after use.*

- For small decorative accessories, such as a display cushion or a bedroom chair cover that will have little wear, fabrics can be chosen for their beauty rather than practicality.

Always buy the best-quality material you can afford, especially for areas that get intense wear, such as sofa covers and window seats. If you are on a tight budget, look for utilitarian fabrics such as ticking, artist's canvas or denim. Closely woven heavy cotton, twill, wool and acrylic mixtures are all suitable for fixed upholstery covers but for loose covers, medium-weight cottons or tougher cotton and polyester mixtures and linen union (a linen/cotton mix) are more suitable materials. Six-ply silk is very durable, too, and can compete with the strongest of upholstery fabrics for upholstering a small ornate chair or sofa. If you want a washable cover, check that the fabric is shrink resistant before you buy.

Choosing patterns and colours

Remember that patterned fabrics almost always have pattern repeats to take into account when you are measuring up and making a seating cover.

A large repeat can be uneconomical, so consider making coordinating items for the same room to use up the fabric remnants. Small geometric prints are easy to accommodate on most furnishings, as are all-over patterns. A print with a central pattern will be less economical for furniture covers, since the dominant pattern should be centred on the seats, backs, arms and on each seat cushion.

It is almost impossible to choose a fabric from a small swatch. Even a colour as simple as ivory

Below *These typically Asian, intricately woven and elaborately dyed fabrics in vibrant colours, are particularly suitable as instant throws for old armchairs or sofas.*

Right *The addition of cushions
makes wooden chairs much more
comfortable. Seat cushions can
be made in varying thicknesses,
according to preference.*

might take on definite hues of pink, yellow or grey
in a large piece, and large patterns are completely
lost on small fabric clippings. Always take as large
a sample of your chosen fabric as possible home
with you before making a major purchase, so that
you can test the colour and strength of design in
the room. (Some retailers may lend you fabric
samples on payment of a deposit.) If you cannot
obtain large samples, buy at least 0.5m (½yd) of
any selected materials to check at home. No colour
will be the same in all lights – or even in different
parts of the same room – so do not expect to get
an exact match. Look for hues and tones that blend
with other fabrics in the room.

Most woven cloths need light thrown on to
them in order to bring out their pattern. Drape,
fold or spread your fabric samples in the position
where they will be used, and look at them at
different times during the day. They might look
quite different in the morning and afternoon and
artificial light can bring further changes.

Furnishing with finished fabrics

Sometimes, fabrics that have already been made
up and destined for one use can be put to another
to make attractive seating covers and throws. With
just a little imagination and confidence many
inexpensive household materials can provide
interesting soft furnishings.

Decorators' dust sheets, for example, are made
from hard-wearing cotton drill, cost very little and,
once laundered, make wonderful raw materials
to be stitched into loose covers. It might be that
you have an old sofa or chair you have inherited
or bought and then found it too expensive to
re-cover. Silk paisley shawls, woollen wraps or
country quilts can be thrown casually over saggy
armchairs to cover areas of wear or to disguise
an ugly fabric beneath. Embroidered crewel work
throws, antique kelims, colourful patterned rugs
or large ethnic blankets and cotton bedcovers
might also make attractive practical, impromptu,
informal sofa covers.

Ideas and projects

ALL FURNITURE deteriorates in time, and all too often it is the fabric on your favourite sofa or set of dining chairs that starts to look faded and shabby or gets stained or torn. But you do not have to discard such furniture just because it is past its best. Drop-in dining seats, for example, can be easily re-covered with a new fabric; old, tired sofas can be revived with loose covers, throws or rugs; mismatched furniture can be disguised with contemporary floor-length covers; and even deck chairs and director's chairs can be given new fabric slings. There are plenty of ideas and projects on the following pages to inspire and encourage you to make your own seats and covers.

Buying old chairs

SECOND-HAND DINING chairs and upholstered furniture in good condition can often be bought at bargain prices, and you can then have fun restoring, repairing, painting, reupholstering or re-covering the chairs using paints and fabrics in colours of your choice.

Finding suitable furniture to cover

If you want a genuine antique, go to a reputable antique shop, unless you are an expert on the subject yourself. If you have the time, visit house sales and auctions. Most have a day's viewing before the auction and you can leave a bid with the sales staff if you are unable to return on the day of the sale itself. This also ensures that sale fever does not tempt you to pay too high a price for your chosen piece! Market stalls and junk shops can often turn up some interesting individual pieces. You can also look through advertisements in the local newspapers for second-hand furniture bargains.

Right *Clean up wooden and painted chair frames before re-covering old seats with new fabric and trimmings to suit your decorating scheme.*

Below *When it comes to buying old wooden chairs, the best bargains are often to be found outside antique shops and second-hand shops.*

What to look for when buying

Make the following checks before buying second-hand furniture, and do not make a purchase if the defects are structural ones that you are not capable of dealing with or not prepared to repair yourself:

- Sit on a chair or sofa to check how comfortable it is.

- Check from the top that the upholstery is still firm. Press down on it; it should spring back into place again. Look at the arms and make sure that they are still secure.

- Look at the underside of upholstered furniture to see if the seat sags, and feel to

make sure that the springs are still in place and attached to the webbing.

- On a dining chair, place one hand on the back and the other on the seat. Then rock it to test for any loose joints or unsteady legs. Creaking may be an indication that it has woodworm. Look for woodworm holes and a sawdust-like deposit. Lots of holes indicate a weakened frame, and a chair that is definitely to be avoided.

Safety point

When buying furniture, try to obtain a guarantee that foam has not been included in it – if foam becomes ignited it can be a smoke and fire hazard. It is illegal in most countries to sell upholstered furniture that has not been tested for fire resistance according to upholstered furniture safety regulations.

Drop-in chair seats

DROP-IN CHAIR SEATS are easy to re-cover at a very low cost. With this type of chair, the seat slips out of the chair, making it simple to work on, and the quantity of material needed is minimal. Use any hard-wearing furnishing fabric, but if you choose one with a large design, the pattern will need to be centred on each chair seat. This is a good time to smarten up the chair frame, too. You can clean and repolish it if it is in good condition, or give it a decorative paint finish to coordinate with your room's colour scheme.

Above *A rich red seat cover highlights the warmth of natural wood on a traditional dining chair. Upholstered chair seats need to be covered in tough, closely woven fabric to withstand extensive wear.*

Re-covering a drop-in chair seat

TOOLS AND MATERIALS

Upholstery-weight furnishing fabric for seat cover (see cutting instructions)

Calico or lining fabric for seat underside (see cutting instructions)

Scissors and tape measure

Old chisel or screwdriver and pincers

Soft pencil

Hammer and 12mm (½in) fine tacks

Tip

Thoroughly clean any upholstered furniture to be re-covered before a new cover is made, otherwise dirt can work through the fibres of the new fabric and damage it.

MEASURING AND CUTTING OUT

Measure the fabric-covered top of the seat from front to back and from side to side. Add 10cm (4in) to each measurement to give the size of the new fabric piece. If you choose a patterned fabric, allow for the design to be centred on the seat. For the cover for the underside, measure the underside and then add a further 5cm (2in) to each measurement. Cut out the fabric pieces.

REMOVING THE OLD COVER

Take out the seat by pushing it upwards. These seats are usually made from a wooden frame, with a base of webbing or ply-wood to hold the wadding or other stuffing. The wadding should be covered with a calico lining and then the main fabric cover. To remove the old cover, turn the seat upside down and gently lever up the tacks with an old chisel or a screwdriver. Remove the tacks with pincers once you can get the pincers under each tack head.

POSITIONING THE NEW FABRIC

Press the main fabric , then fold it in half lengthways, wrong sides facing, and mark the fold line in pencil. Repeat, folding the fabric in half widthways. Mark corresponding centre points along each side of the seat on

the underside of the frame. Lay out the fabric, wrong side up, and position the frame on top, lining up the centre point marks on fabric and frame.

TACKING THE COVER IN PLACE

Pull the fabric fairly taut and partially hammer in one tack at each marked central position to hold the fabric in place. Turn the seat over and check from the top side that the cover is positioned accurately. Adjust if necessary, then add more temporary tacks (see page 19) at 2.5cm (1in) intervals along each side.

FIXING THE CORNERS

Stretch the fabric taut diagonally at each corner and put a temporary tack through

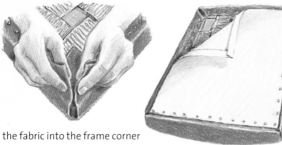

the fabric into the frame corner to hold it. Ensure that the amount of loose fabric each side of the corner is equal and fold each piece into a pleat as illustrated. Before fixing down, trim away any excess fabric beneath the pleat, leaving no more than a 1cm (³⁄₈in) turn. Tack the pleats down. Check the fit from the top side, adjust the tacks if necessary then hammer them all home.

COVERING THE UNDERSIDE

Turn under 3cm (1¼in) along all the sides of the fabric for the underside of the seat and press. Place the fabric, right side up on the underside of the seat, positioning it centrally to cover all the raw edges of the seat's main fabric. Tack firmly in position at about 2.5cm (1in) intervals on all four sides.

TO FINISH CUT-OUT CORNERS

Pull the fabric taut diagonally, as for ordinary covers, and then fix a tack temporarily in the centre of each cut-out on the underside of the seat. Pleat the fabric carefully at each outer corner and then tack down as before.

Below *Traditionally shaped balloon-back dining chairs are given a modern look with white paint and checked fabric seats.*

Temporary tacking

To ensure a professional finish, tack the cover temporarily first. To do this, drive the tacks in only partially, just far enough to hold the fabric in place, then at each stage turn the seat the right way up to check that the design remains accurately centred. The fabric grain should run straight in each direction, and the cover should be smoothly taut but not pulled so tight that the tack points show. Once you are wholly satisfied with the finished effect, tack the cover firmly into position, using a small pin hammer.

Above *Bold plaid fabric gives this old carver chair a crisp look. A group of different chairs can be matched up by painting them all the same colour and covering their seats with the same fabric.*

Over-stuffed chair seats

AN OVER-STUFFED SEAT is an upholstered seat that is fixed permanently to the frame, its fabric wrapping over the edge of it. On an over-stuffed seat, unlike a drop-in seat, you need to work from the top side of the chair, so it is easy to check that any design remains centred and that the grain of the fabric runs straight from front to back and across the chair. Use any upholstery-weight furnishing fabric but ensure that you buy enough material if you have chosen a bold design so that the pattern can be centred on each chair that you cover.

Covering an over-stuffed chair seat

TOOLS AND MATERIALS

Upholstery-weight furnishing fabric for seat cover (see cutting instructions)

Calico or lining fabric for seat lining (see cutting instructions)

Cotton wadding

Braid

Scissors and tape measure

Old chisel or screwdriver and pincers

Craft knife

Hammer and 12mm (½in) fine tacks

Fabric adhesive

MEASURING AND CUTTING OUT

Measure the fabric-covered top of the seat from front to back and from side to side. Add 10cm (4in) to each measurement for the size of the new fabric piece to allow for a 5cm (2in) deep seat, or more for a bigger chair. If you choose a patterned fabric allow for the design to be centred on the seat.

For the lining, add 5cm (2in) all round to the seat top size. For the wadding, add 2cm (¾in) all round to the seat top size. For the braid, measure all four sides of the chair seat and add 5cm (2in) for turnings.

Cut out all the necessary pieces and press the fabric.

REMOVING THE OLD COVER AND LINING

Pull away the old braid. Using a chisel or screwdriver, gently lever up the tacks holding the end of braid and the old cover to the frame, then get the pincers under each tack head to remove it. Discard the old wadding lying between the lining and the top cover, then remove the lining in the same way as the top cover.

REPLACING THE LINING AND WADDING

Fit the lining piece (cut 5cm/2in larger than the seat top on all sides), following the next two steps for positioning and fixing the top cover. Make small, evenly spaced pleats at the front corners. Trim away the excess lining with a craft knife. Place the wadding (cut slightly larger than the seat top) over the lining.

POSITIONING THE TOP COVER

Place the main seat fabric (cut 5cm/2in larger than the seat top on all sides) over the seat, centring any pattern. Partially hammer in one tack in the centre of each chair side edge and at the front to hold the cover temporarily in position (see 'Temporary tacking', page 19).

FIXING THE BACK CORNERS

Fold the main seat fabric forward to line up with the chair back struts and make one cut from each fabric back corner to within 1cm (³⁄₈in) of each upright strut. Turn under the raw edges, trim the excess fabric, fold under again and fit neatly around each strut. Tack down. Hammer in tacks all along the sides and back of the seat, so that they are spaced at about 2.5cm (1in) intervals.

Below *A stylish period feel is created with this traditional frame and over-stuffed chair seat cover in green and gold fabric with coordinating trim.*

FIXING THE FRONT CORNERS

Either use a double pleat on the front corners (see 'Fixing the corners', page 17) or, for a squarer corner, use a single pleat. Fix a temporary tack to hold the fabric near the corner on the side edge, then fold the fabric around towards the front edge and tack here after cutting away any surplus fabric along the edge. Fold the extra fabric under to form a neat single pleat on the corner. Cut away any surplus fabric below the pleat and fix in place with two tacks. Tack the front edge down. Make sure that all the tacks are knocked in and then trim the fabric close to the tacks.

ADDING THE EDGING BRAID

Turn under 1cm (³⁄₈in) at one end of the braid and tack it beside one back strut, lining it up so that it goes over the raw edge of the cover. Add adhesive to the wrong side of the braid and over the tacked edge of the cover; press the braid down all along the cover edge. At the opposite

Upholstery tips

- If, on removing an old seat cover, you find that the upholstery beneath is in poor condition, replace this before fitting the new cover. In most areas local upholstery classes are available and are led by an expert upholsterer who will oversee you through all the stages of replacing the webbing and springs, and fixing the stuffing.

- Temporary tacking (see page 19) allows you to make any adjustments so that you can be sure the cover is positioned accurately and fits smoothly before all the tacks are finally driven home.

back strut, turn under the other end of braid and glue in place. Cover the back edge similarly.

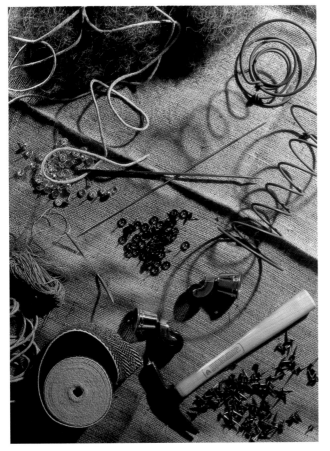

Opposite left *The chair on the left is lined and ready for covering with either a fixed cover or a slip-on style with a gathered skirt – as on the chair on the right.*

Left *Reupholstering furniture requires specific tools and materials. It is a specialist skill and one worth learning at an upholstery class if you intend making a hobby of restoring old furniture.*

Dressed-up dining chairs

SURFACE-WORN or unattractive-looking upright chairs can be transformed with slip-over floor-length fabric covers made from a series of squares and rectangles. Whether the chairs are upholstered, or made entirely of wood or even metal, a set of similarly dressed dining chairs can look very stylish in a room setting carefully designed to coordinate with them. Besides teaming the dressed-up chairs with the usual soft furnishings of curtains or blinds, and with flooring and wall colours, you can easily coordinate the fabric used for your dressed-up dining chairs with the table linen for an impressive table setting.

Dressing an upright chair

TOOLS AND MATERIALS

Closely woven furnishing fabric for main cover (see cutting instructions)

Contrasting fabric for lining skirt and false corner pleats (see cutting instructions)

Pencil and paper

Brown paper

Scissors and sewing equipment

Matching sewing thread

> **Tip**
> Wallpaper lining paper is a good, strong alternative to brown paper for making paper patterns.

The cover shown opposite fits the chair back and seat, and has a smart straight-sided skirt with a false pleat at each corner. The skirt sections are lined with a contrasting fabric, which is used for the false pleats that peep out between the skirt sections. The instructions given below are for a straightforward cover, which can easily be dressed up using one or more of the ideas featured under 'Optional decorative extras' (see page 25), some of which are illustrated.

MEASURING UP

Using pencil and paper, draw a rough sketch of the chair to be covered and mark on it the measurements given below, always measuring each section at its widest or longest point. Add 5cm (2in) to the back and seat measurements to allow for adjustment when fitting, and 2.5cm (1in) for seam allowances. Remember that if you choose a design with a large motif this will need to be centred and matched up on each of the six main sections of the cover, so

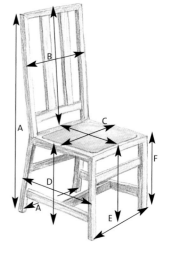

allow extra material for this (this is unnecessary on the skirt lining pieces).

- OUTSIDE BACK COVER (A): Measure the chair back width and the length from the top edge to the floor. Measure from the seat to the floor for the back panel lining (AA).

- INSIDE BACK COVER (B): Measure the width including the frame sides, and the length from the top back edge to the seat.

fabric section (D), 12mm (½in) from the raw edges along the sides and bottom. Repeat on the second side panel and the front panel (E). Attach the back skirt lining (AA) to the lower back panel section (A) in the same way, stitching the sides as far as 2.5cm (1in) from the lining's top raw edge. Turn under a 12mm (½in) hem along the lining's top edge and slipstitch in place to the outer back panel when the fabric is turned the right side out. Trim the bottom corners on the skirt pieces, turn the fabric the right side out and press.

LINING THE FALSE CORNER PLEATS

With right sides facing, pin, baste and stitch two false corner pleat pieces together along the sides and lower edges as for the skirt sections. Repeat with the remaining six pleat pieces to make the other three corner pleats. Finish, trim, press and turn the right side out as for the skirt sections.

- SEAT (C): Measure the seat from the frame edge each time, from side to side and from back to front.

- SIDE PANELS × 2 (D): Measure from the top of the seat frame to the floor and from the outer edge of the back leg to the outer edge of the front leg.

- FRONT PANEL (E): Measure from the top of the seat frame to the floor and the width from the outer edge of one front leg to the other.

- FALSE CORNER PLEATS (F): Measure from the seat frame top to the floor and cut each piece 23cm (9in) wide.

CUTTING OUT THE COVER

Make pattern pieces of each section from brown paper, label them and arrange pieces A to E on the main fabric. Check that each section follows the straight grain of the fabric and that any pattern motifs are centred. When you are happy with the arrangement and have ensured that the design matches on all sections, pin each pattern piece in place and cut out. From the lining, cut two side panels (D), one front panel (E), one short outer back panel (AA) and eight false corner pleat pieces (F).

LINING THE SKIRT PIECES

With right sides facing, pin, baste then stitch one skirt side panel lining piece to the top

place to fit, ensuring that the seam runs along the outer back edge of the frame. Make a small dart in the inside back piece at each of the top back corners to fit the frame shape. Remove the fabric and stitch the darts. Trim the raw edges outside the seam line to 12mm (½in), then stitch the two back sections to each other along the top and sides. Neaten the raw edges.

ADDING THE SEAT AND SKIRT

Replace the back sections on the chair and pin the seat section (C), wrong side uppermost, to the inside chair back (B) along the back edge. Add the side (D) and front (E) skirt pieces, the lining outwards, and pin to the seat

FITTING THE BACK SECTIONS ON THE CHAIR

With the wrong sides facing outwards, place the outside back (A) and inside back (B) sections together on the chair. Pin in

section so that the seam runs along the outer frame edge and the skirt edges meet at the back and front leg corners. Remove, trim the seat seams, if necessary and baste all pinned seams.

Optional decorative extras

- Use some ribbon or make matching fabric ties (see page 44) for highlighting corner pleats or for tying across the back of a chair.

- On a chair with a shaped back include side openings and use bow ties or touch-and-close fastening to hold the cover closed.

- Add a seat cushion made to match the chair cover. Alternatively, simply enhance comfort by tying a flattish square cushion to the seat beneath the cover.

- To add a border along the bottom edge of the cover skirt sections, as seen in this project (see right), cut four strips of lining fabric 7.5cm (3in) wide by the length of each skirt side plus 2cm (¾in) for turnings. Press under the raw edge by 1cm (⅜in) on all sides of each strip and topstitch in place on the skirt sections.

- Piping can be made from the contrasting lining fabric and added to the back and seat edge seams for an additional effect.

POSITIONING THE FALSE PLEATS

Position a lined pleat section centrally over each skirt corner. Pin and baste in place along the seam line through all the layers. Stitch the seams and neaten the raw edges. Press the seams, turn the cover the right side out, press and slip in place over the chair back.

Left *An optional decorative touch is to add long floppy bows in matching fabric to chair backs.*

Above right *Button-through covers and short seat frills liven up the appearance of these chairs with upholstered seats and backs.*

Right *An old set of wooden dining chairs has been updated with close-fitting covers in white waffle-weave cotton; the same fabric has been used as a tablecloth, beneath the glass top that covers the dining table.*

Loose covers

TRADITIONAL LOOSE COVERS are not fixed to the furniture they cover, but form a second skin to upholstered furniture, following its shape and contours closely; they are not actually as loose as the name might imply.

Loose covers can be used to provide a new look for old and worn, but still comfortable, sofas and chairs. You can use loose covers to protect a special upholstered finish from dust, general wear and damage from enthusiastic children and pets. They are also useful for when you want a colour scheme change. They are not difficult to make and can be removed easily for cleaning. However, no cover can be made to sit neatly over furniture with shiny finishes such as leather and plastic.

Choosing fabric for loose covers

Use only upholstery-weight or loose-cover fabric for making a loose cover. This is crease-resistant, firmly woven and tough so it is able to withstand the wear demanded of it. Linen union and cotton damask are good choices. Thick or heavy fabric is unsuitable as it is difficult to sew, particularly where piping is included in the seams, and where a number of layers of fabric must be stitched together. If the covers are to be washed, check that the fabric is colour-fast and non-shrink.

Using piping

Piping shows off the shape of furniture and can be made in the same fabric or in a contrasting colour to make a feature of it. Not only does piping give a professional finish, it also strengthens the seams. If the fabric used for the piping is not the same as the main fabric it must be similar in weight and texture and as good a quality as the main fabric since the piped edges of covers wear quickly.

Plain or patterned fabric?

Plain fabrics look smart, especially if the seams are

Right *Two identical armchairs are given completely different looks with the help of loose covers. The one on the right has a country look with its loose cover in a floral fabric and a piped and gathered skirt. The tailored box pleats used on the other chair look smart and modern, yet blend well with the country-look fabric.*

Above *Since the arms are often the first areas on an armchair or sofa to show signs of wear, fitted covers can be made for the arms only, rather than for the whole piece of furniture. This is easier and more economical with fabric.*

Left *The slip-over cream-coloured cover for this armchair complements the rustic feel of the setting provided by the adjacent wooden seat and the flagstone floor.*

Above *Plain fabrics make smart-looking loose covers and are more economical than patterned fabrics since there is no need to allow extra material for matching patterns.*

Trimming options

Deep bullion fringing is an alternative to a frill around the bottom of a loose cover. Other shop-bought braids and trimmings are possible options. However, do bear in mind how your covers will be cleaned and whether such trimmings are suitable.

outlined with contrasting coloured piping; they also make economic sense when it comes to fabric quantities. Fabric with a small random design is similarly economical and easy to work with, since it does not require careful pattern matching. In addition, fabric with a small pattern is a good choice since it disguises dirty marks more easily. Bold motifs, checks and stripes look effective but require more care and extra fabric as designs need to be centred and matched both up and down and across the furniture.

Style of openings

Loose cover openings are traditionally held closed with a long, tough zip but alternative choices are touch-and-close fastening, press-stud fastening tape or hook-and-eye tape (see page 70). If you want to make a feature of the opening, use bow ties, which can be repeated on the opposite back and the front corners for decorative effect (see pages 34–37), or use colourful buttons and fabric or cord tabs.

Skirt design choices

The simplest loose covers are held beneath the furniture with a casing and tape or cord ties; this design suits modern straight-sided sofas with long legs and traditional chairs with ornate legs. Skirts give furniture an attractive finish and are useful for hiding unsightly legs. A tailored skirt with corner pleats gives a classic look, while box pleats or a gathered skirt blend well with country-look fabrics and furniture styles. For a more unusual skirt, consider the two-tier effect of a double frill or a straight, tailored design with a scalloped-over skirt.

Making a loose cover for a sofa

TOOLS AND MATERIALS

Loose-cover furnishing fabric for cover (see cutting instructions)

Pencil and paper

Scissors and sewing equipment

Tailor's chalk or small sticky labels

Ready-made piping (optional – see page 67)

Matching sewing thread

Zip, touch-and-close or press-stud fastening tape (optional)

Loose covers are not difficult to make but for a successful result they require careful and frequent fitting before the sections are finally sewn together. The trick is to work directly on the sofa or armchair that you are covering , working with the fabric inside out so that you can adjust the seams easily. Loose covers can have a well-fitting tailored look and closely resemble upholstered furniture, or they can have a more casual unstructured look.

MEASURING UP

Using pencil and paper, draw a rough sketch of the sofa to be covered and mark on it the dimensions of each section as you measure it. Always measure each section at its widest or longest point, and add 10cm (4in) to each measurement to allow for seams and adjustments. Also allow extra fabric – an extra 15cm (6in) to the inside back, back and sides of seat and inside arm sections – for tucking in around the seat to hold the cover in place. In addition, add an allowance for pattern matching, and remember to consider any seat cushions that need to be re-covered.

CUTTING OUT

Cut out squares and rectangles from the fabric to correspond to these measurements, checking that the pieces you cut have the

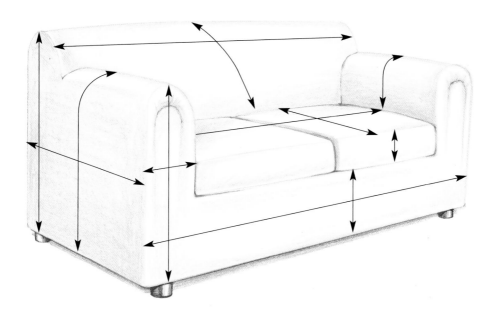

straight grain of the fabric running up and down the chair and from front to back across the seat. As you cut out each piece of fabric, mark the wrong side with tailor's chalk or use small sticky labels to indicate its intended position. This will help you assemble the pieces when you come to pin the cover together.

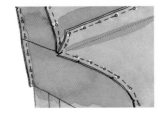

Below *A comfortable sofa gets a new look with a pale-coloured loose cover. Piping accentuates the boxed seat cushions, while squashy pillows and colourful scatter cushions add comfort and splashes of colour.*

ASSEMBLING THE COVER

With the wrong side of the fabric facing outwards and following the lines of the sofa, pin the pieces to the sofa and to each other for an accurate fit. Make darts if necessary to take in any excess fullness on the inside pieces, but make sure the cover will slip off easily. Then mark the seam lines using tailor's chalk. Remove the cover, and baste the seams with large firm stitches. Before trimming the fabric to

2.5cm (1in) seam allowances and machine stitching the seams, sit on the sofa to make sure you have allowed enough material so that the seams are not strained excessively.

FINISHING OFF

Machine stitch along the basted seams, including piping in the seams if required (see 'Optional finishes', right). Leave an opening along one back corner

seam for taking the cover on and off, if necessary, for fastening with a zip or touch-and-close or press-stud fastening tape (see page 70). Press seams and snip curves where necessary. Neaten the opening and the lower edge to finish, making sure that the hem along the lower edge hangs evenly just above floor level.

To make a false hem using concealed piping, smooth the loose cover into position on the sofa, the right side out. Trim the lower unfinished edge all round and baste piping to the right side of the fabric. Remove the cover and machine stitch the piping in place. Press the piping down then stitch the seam to the wrong side of the fabric.

Optional finishes

- For a tailored look, attach piping (see page 67) in the same colour or a contrasting one along the seams to emphasize the shape of the sofa. Attach this after pinning the cover panels together by removing a few pins at a time to insert the piping between the panels of fabric.

- To make a simple gathered frill to fit around the bottom of the sofa, measure around the bottom edge of the finished loose cover. Prepare a strip of fabric for the frill, its length 1½ times this measurement. The width of the frill will depend on the size and type of sofa and should finish 12mm (½in) above the floor (remember to allow for turnings). Prepare, gather and attach the frill to the cover according to the instructions on pages 68–69.

- A cover can be tied beneath a chair or sofa to keep it in place. For this you need to allow extra fabric for making a draw-string casing along the bottom edge through which to thread tape that can be tied around each leg.

Left *A Victorian chair covered in classic red and white fabric adds comfort to a bathroom. The frilled skirt is short, allowing the shapely legs to be displayed.*

Slip-over chair cover with ties

TOOLS AND MATERIALS

Loose-cover furnishing fabric
for cover, seat cushion and ties
(see cutting instructions)

Pencil and paper

Brown paper

Tailor's chalk

Scissors and sewing equipment

Matching sewing thread

This semi-fitted chair cover
simply slips over the chair like
an egg cosy. The inverted pleats
on each back corner allow for
this and bow ties along the pleat
lines hold the cover neatly in
place and help provide some
extra decoration. The chair cover
drops to just above floor level
and is finished with a plain
hemmed edge.

Below *This chair cover, in
fabric to match the floor-length
curtains, simply slips over the
upholstery and ties in place easily
down its back corners.*

MEASURING UP

Using pencil and paper, roughly sketch the chair to be covered and note the measurements given below, measuring each section of the chair carefully at its widest or longest point. Add an extra 5cm (2in) to all the measurements to allow for any necessary adjustment when fitting the cover. Also remember to leave an extra 2.5cm (1in) for the seam allowances.

Note: some chairs, such as the one illustrated here, require a tuck-in between the back and inside arm edges.

- OUTSIDE BACK COVER: Measure the chair back width and the length from the top edge to the floor.

- INSIDE BACK COVER: Measure the width and the length from the top back edge to the seat. Add an extra 15cm (6in) to the length for the seat tuck-in.

- SEAT: Measure from side to side and from back to front. Add an extra 30cm (12in) to both measurements for the seat tuck-in.

- LOWER FRONT SECTION: Measure the chair width and the drop from the seat front edge to the floor.

- INSIDE ARMS: Measure the width and length at the

widest and longest points. Add an extra 15cm (6in) to the length for the seat tuck-in. If your chair has arms with gussets along the top and side edges, you will need to measure, fit and stitch these as separate sections.

- OUTSIDE ARMS: Measure the width and length at the widest and longest points.

- INVERTED BACK CORNER PLEATS: Use the outside back cover length measurement and make two gusset strips to this length and 25cm (10in) wide.

- BOW TIES: Make each strip 7.5cm (3in) wide by 33cm (13in) long and make enough pairs to space them evenly every 12.5–15cm (5–6in) down each back corner pleated edge.

- SEAT CUSHION: See page 37.

CUTTING OUT THE PATTERN PIECES

Using the measurements calculated as above, cut out pattern pieces of each main section from brown paper and label them with their section name as you work. Place the pattern pieces on the chair and pin them together, starting with the outer back and arms, then add the inner back and the other sections. Make folds in the paper

around curves as necessary and slip the tuck-ins in place. Pencil in the fitting lines. Remove the pattern pieces from the chair and cut the paper to follow curves, allowing an extra 7.5cm (3in) outside the pencilled seam lines for accurate fitting and seam allowances.

CUTTING OUT THE COVER

Arrange the pattern pieces on the fabric, making sure that any fabric design lines up as necessary. Pin the pattern pieces in place and cut out the fabric. Also include the corner pleat, seat cushion and bow tie pieces in the layout.

FITTING THE COVER PIECES

With the wrong side of the fabric facing outwards, pin all the main fabric sections to each other on the chair, making any minor adjustments where you think them necessary so that they fit well. Then mark in all the seam lines on the fabric using the tailor's chalk. Remove all the fabric sections from the chair

and trim the seam allowances to 2.5cm (1in). Neaten all the raw edges.

ATTACHING THE CORNER PLEAT PIECES

With right sides together, pin, baste and stitch one gusset strip down one outer back edge. Pin the opposite edge of the gusset piece to the outer back edge of the side panel and stitch. Temporarily remove adjoining pinned pieces to make stitching

easier. Repeat to stitch the second gusset strip to the other back corner. With right sides together, fold the gusset in half along its length, and pin in place through the seam lines. Stitch along the seam line for 5cm (2in) down from the top raw edge. Open out and centre the pleat at the back of this seam. Pin, then stitch across the top edge as shown to hold the pleat. Press.

STITCHING THE COVER

Repin the fabric pieces together where necessary and machine stitch to join all the cover sections along the marked lines. Press the seams open and replace the cover on the chair, right side out.

HEMMING THE COVER

Turn the fabric under and pin a double hem along the lower edge of the cover, making sure that the hem edge hangs just above floor level. When the length is correct, remove the cover and stitch the hem.

MAKING AND FITTING THE TIES

With the wrong side uppermost, fold one long edge of one strip to its centre and press. Repeat along the opposite side so that the raw edges meet. Press 12mm (½in) to the wrong side across one short end; leave the other short end of the tie unfinished. With the fabric's right side facing outwards, fold the strip in half along its length.

Press well. Stitch close to all the edges. Repeat to make all the ties. Mark the tie positions along the back corner seams, spacing them equally 12.5–15cm (5–6in) apart. Unpick the seam at each point and insert 2.5cm (1in) of the raw end of each tie. Stitch the seam again to hold the tie ends in place. Replace the cover on the chair and tie the bows.

COVERING THE SEAT CUSHION

Follow the cutting out and making up instructions detailed opposite to cover the seat cushion. Remember to make sure that the pattern on the cushion matches that on the chair cover.

Above *A close-up of the opening shows the gusset and the bow ties that hold this decorative slip-over cover in place.*

Re-covering a seat cushion

Measure each face of the seat cushion (top, bottom and the four sides) and cut a panel of fabric for each, adding a 2.5cm (1in) seam allowance around each panel.

Position the four gusset pieces, wrong side out, along the side faces of the cushion. Pin the seams at the corners. Remove from the cushion and stitch the corner seams. The seam length should match the cushion depth only and not extend into the seam allowance. Trim the seam allowances and press the seams open.

Reposition the stitched gusset around the cushion, wrong side outwards, and lay the top panel over the cushion, wrong side uppermost. Pin this panel to the gusset all around the edges. Turn the cushion over and repeat for the bottom panel, leaving one edge open so that you can remove the cover. Stitch all the pinned seams. Trim the seam allowances and trim all excess fabric from the corners. Press the fabric, turning under and pressing the seam allowances along the open edge. Turn the cushion cover the right side out and push out the corners neatly using the tip of a pair of scissors.

Insert the cushion (unpick the gusset seams at the opening if the cushion is too thick or firm to insert easily). Slipstitch the opening closed, if you are prepared to unpick this whenever the cushion cover needs removing for cleaning. Alternatively, use a zip or touch-and-close or press-stud fastening tape (see page 70).

Instant cover-ups

IF YOU ARE SHORT of time, tight for cash, or prefer a casual furnishing effect, then a 'no-sew' throw-over cover is a simple way to give a sofa or upholstered chair a new lease of life. Where over-exuberant children and pets cause problems for favourite furniture, throws also provide a quick method of protection and can be cleverly used to hide the damage from a cat's sharp claws. They can also add zest to a too-bland colour scheme in a room or help to create an easy change of look between summer and winter.

Cover-up options

Throws for use over armchairs and sofas are widely available in a huge range of designs and fabrics and you are not restricted to using only bedspreads and blankets. Consider using a beautiful antique shawl or an embroidered tablecloth; exotic rugs that are too precious to cover the floor or cotton rag rugs stay in place well on furniture, too. Lengths of fabric can be joined together to make an all-embracing cover or you can use a decorative flat sheet that falls in graceful folds around a chair base. More texture can be added by outlining the chosen textiles with braid or a fringe or by adding decorative corner tassels.

Make a lightly padded throw by stitching together two large panels of suitable furnishing fabric as though making a cushion cover and inserting a layer of fleece, wadding or

interlining between the layers. Turn the fabric the right side out and machine stitch parallel lines of stitching along its length to hold the layers together.

How much you want a throw-over cover to overhang a sofa or chair and how much you tuck in depends on the style of the furniture and of its setting. The disadvantage of throw-over covers is that regular smoothing is required to maintain a neat finish. Smoothing the cover over the chair or sofa and pushing it into the gaps around the seat helps keep it looking tidier for longer when in use.

Taking measurements

To work out the size of an all-enveloping throw-over cover, measure the chair or sofa from the floor at the back to the floor at the front, following the curves of the furniture. Then add about

Above *A cream-coloured throw looks modern and stylish and is the perfect foil for assorted scatter cushions.*

Left *A large bedspread acts as an all-enveloping throw on a sofa to hide wear, damage or stains.*

Below *An attractive bedspread saves a shabby-looking armchair that is structurally sound. A quick way to lift the bedspread off the floor behind the chair is to bunch the fabric and secure it with elastic bands to make two large 'rosettes' of fabric.*

Above *Draping fabrics, shawls and bedspreads over sofas can bring a soft, luxurious element into your home.*

30cm (12in) extra for every tuck-in that you want. Do the same from side to side, adding 60cm (24in) for the two tuck-ins – one on either side of the seat.

Alternative effects

Quick cover-ups can let you create a very individual look. Here are some ideas that can start you experimenting:

- SIMPLY DRAPED
  A quick, stylish effect is gained by literally throwing soft draping fabric over a sofa or chair. Adding scatter cushions or placing a seat

cushion on top of the throw helps to keep it in position.

- SCULPTURED FINISH
  A number of small rugs can be used to follow a sofa's shape. Use one over the sofa back and another over the seat, tucking the rug sides into the space behind the seat cushions to help pin them in place. You could add a further couple, draping one over each arm. Choose rug shades that blend for a subtle effect, or pick strongly contrasting colours to create a focal point.

- THE LAYERED LOOK
  This is a much more casual effect, which is created with rugs or a range of textiles draped, angled and folded over back, arms and seat to give a patchwork of shapes and colours.

- USING TIES
  Fabric can be draped on furniture and the corners tied in place either side with fabric ties or ribbon, or the fabric can be swathed around a chair and tied in the lower centre front or at the back. Or use contrasting-coloured cords to encircle the back and base of a fabric-covered sofa or chair. If the fabric is soft enough you may be able to tie the excess fabric in a large knot, to one side of a chair for example or around its legs.

- TAKING A TUCK
  A large sheet or bedspread can be tucked in to give a neat, structured look to furniture. Lay your chosen material over a sofa from back to front, smoothing it over and tucking it in both behind and in front of the seat cushions as well as along the sides. Extend the tucks as pleats over the back and then secure in place with a few stitches where necessary. Slim strips of foam pushed into the tuck-in spaces around the cushions help keep the cover in place.

Tip
For most styles of sofa, whether you are making a loose cover or a throw for a cover-up, you will have to join widths of fabric to make up the full width of the required panels. To join widths of fabric as inconspicuously as possible, try to stitch them together so that the seams correspond with the edges of the seat cushions.

Below *A throw in colours to coordinate with the sofa and placed over the seat cushions only can protect them from small children and pets while still looking classy.*

Ties for covers and cushions

RIBBON, BRAID, CORD or purpose-made fabric ties can all be used to hold soft furnishings in place in a number of practical and decorative ways or they can appear simply as a design feature. Various styles of indoor and outdoor furniture have metal, plastic or wooden frames around which ties can be used. Ties can be used in an obvious manner to secure loose covers (see page 34) and seat cushions (see below) or can be used unobtrusively, for example to secure a loose cover underneath a sofa with ties around the castors or furniture legs.

Tie-on chair cushion

MATERIALS

Fabric for cushion covers – approximately 60cm (⅝yd) of 120cm (48in) wide fabric for each chair

Brown paper and pencil

Scissors and sewing equipment

Cotton ribbon or braid for ties – 1.2m (1¼yd) of 1.5cm (⅝in) wide ribbon or braid per chair

Matching sewing thread

4 plastic or metal press-stud fastenings

Cushion pad to fit finished cover or sheet foam, 2cm (¾in) thick, cut to size

This tie-on cushion can be adapted to suit a wide variety of chairs. You could make all the cushions for a set of chairs in matching fabrics or use a different plain fabric for each seat. Fill the covers with conventional cushion pads or sheet foam cut to size (use the paper template of the chair seat without the seam allowance – see Step 1). Use linen or cotton in plain, woven or printed designs. Avoid fabric with very large repeat

Right *Braid gives a pretty decorative edging to this simple tie-on cushion in a plain cream-coloured fabric.*

designs, which will result in wastage if you are making a set of cushions. Cushion covers can be piped (see page 67) and/or decorated with a frill (see box, below) if liked.

width of the template and 5cm (2in) wide to make a facing.

MAKING THE CHAIR SEAT TEMPLATE

Place the brown paper on top of the chair seat and draw around it in pencil to make the template for the top panel of the cushion cover. Add 1.5cm (⅝in) all round for seam allowances. Use the same pattern for the bottom panel, adding an extra 5cm (2in) depth to the back edge to allow for a turning.

CUTTING OUT

Cut out two panels of fabric using the template, positioning the template centrally over any pattern motif in the fabric. Cut a strip of fabric to match the

POSITIONING THE TIES

Halve the length of ribbon or braid. Neaten the raw ends if necessary then fold each piece in half. Pin the ribbons to the right side of the top panel of the cushion cover, with their folded edge almost meeting the raw

Adding a frill

A tie-on cushion cover needs two separate lengths of frill so as to fit around the back struts of the chair. Cut two strips of fabric, 15cm (6in) wide – one strip 1½ times the length of the back edge of the seat, the other strip 1½ times the total length of the remaining three sides (join lengths if necessary to make the frill long enough).

Prepare each frill strip (see pages 68–69) and stitch gathering stitches 1cm (⅜in) from the raw edges.

Position the ties on the top cushion cover panel as before, before adding the frills. Gather the short strip to fit across the cover's back edge, excluding the seam allowance. Pin to the

right side of the top panel, raw edges matching, leaving the 1.5cm (⅝in) seam allowance free at each end. Gather the second strip and pin around the other three sides of the panel in the same way, allowing extra fullness at the corners so the frill will hang neatly. Stitch in place 1.5cm (⅝in) from the raw edges. Complete the facing and cushion cover as in the main text.

back edge but 6mm (¼in) from it and 2.5cm (1in) in from the sides of the back corners.

POSITIONING THE FACING

Turn under and stitch a double, 12mm (½in) wide hem along one long edge of the facing strip. Position the strip across the back edge of the top panel, over the ribbons, with right sides facing and raw edges matching. Stitch in place, taking a 1.5cm (⅝in) seam and catching the two pinned ribbon lengths within the seams. Turn the facing over to the wrong side of the fabric and press.

FINISHING THE BOTTOM PANEL

Turn under a 2.5cm (1in) double hem along the back edge of the bottom panel. Topstitch in place.

MAKING UP THE COVER

With right sides together, pin, baste and stitch around the three edges of the seat cover, catching in the sides of the facing and leaving the back edge open. Trim the seam allowance and clip diagonally across the corners of the cover. Turn the cover to the right side and press.

FINISHING THE BACK OPENING

Sew the stud part of the press studs along the bottom panel's edge. Sew the socket parts to the facing along the edge of the top panel. Insert a cushion pad or sheet foam cut to size.

Above *A simple square cushion tied to the chair frame adds a touch of comfort to the seat.*

Making fabric ties

Cut strips of fabric for the number of ties and to the desired width and length. Fold each strip in half lengthways, right sides facing, and run some tape or cord along the length, close to the fold. Stitch across one end, catching the end of the tape in the seam. Then stitch along the long edge of each tie, taking a 1.5cm (5⁄8in) seam and taking care not to catch the tape in the seam. Trim the seam allowance and pull the tape to turn the fabric the right side out. Trim away the tape, press each tie, then turn in the raw edges and slipstitch the opening.

For narrower fabric ties make rouleaux instead. Cut strips of fabric to the length required and about 2.5cm (1in) wide. Turn under the short ends then turn under 6mm (1⁄4in) down each long edge; fold in half, right side facing outwards. Stitch along the middle of the strip to enclose all the raw edges.

Types of ties

Neatened, stitched strips of fabric and assorted synthetic, cotton or silk ribbons, cords and braids are suitable as ties for soft furnishings. They can be stitched directly to fabric or used in conjunction with metal eyelets to tie seat and back cushions or loose covers to metal, plastic or wooden chairs or benches. Ties can also make a colourful contribution and should be long enough to knot or tie in a bow around the seat frame.

Fabric ties are easily made (see box, left) and require little fabric. Some ribbons and braids need their raw edges turning and neatening to prevent fraying. Check that the material you use for the ties is washable, colour-fast and non-shrinking.

Right *A pretty, floral chintz seat cover for a bamboo chair is fixed with long ties of silky ribbon.*

Above and right top *Create broad, bold and bountiful bows of ribbon, or slim bootlace fixings for fastening covers to furniture.*

THERE IS A degree of overlap between seating and soft furnishings for use indoors and out. Wrought-iron or wicker furniture, director's chairs and wooden benches, for example, could all feature equally well in the garden or inside the house, in a conservatory or garden room perhaps. Similarly, throws, tie-on cushions, bolsters and bench mattresses work inside or out, instantly softening wooden- or metal-framed furniture or moulded plastic chairs – both decoratively and in terms of comfort. A simple tie-on seat cover for a foldaway bistro chair can be used to introduce interest, colour and decoration to a terrace or conservatory, while a plain garden bench can be painted and dressed with a fabric-covered seat and tasselled bolsters to create an elegant and inviting seat in a garden room. You can turn a small patio or backyard into a summer dining room; a sunny terrace can add an instant extension to a living room, or a secret bower in a quiet corner of the garden can become an escape from the world.

Using pattern and colour

Inspiration for colour and pattern in soft furnishings for indoor/outdoor seating may be drawn from many sources – from the flowers and plants in pots on the terrace or growing in the garden, or from mementoes and photographs from foreign holidays where more tropical climates can be reflected in a bolder use of design and colour.

Prints and patterns for soft furnishing fabrics used indoors may reflect the outdoors with delicate botanical motifs, floral and topiary designs. Outdoor soft furnishings may be made to

complement an existing interior decorating scheme that is simply carried out on to the terrace. Alternatively, since outdoor furniture is used only occasionally for entertaining, it lends itself to more adventurous use of colour and pattern and can be used to introduce different textures not usually seen inside the home. Choose schemes to blend with your furniture – bright patterns can liven up moulded plastic furniture, while bold stripes are ideal for deck chairs and director's chairs.

Left *Since there are less restraints on fabric colours and patterns outside you can be more adventurous. Big frilly cushions in bold stripes soften the outline of these wrought-iron chairs, while colourful panels of fabric make a temporary awning, offering protection from the sun.*

Above right *An iron bench subtly links inside to outside with its cushions covered in a delicate floral print.*

Right *Whether your outdoor space is a large garden, a small patio or a roof terrace, deck chairs and director's chairs are ideal as they can be easily folded and stored away out of season. You can cover them yourself with fabric of your choice and make cushions to match or contrast.*

Setting the scene outdoors

Use your garden or terrace as an extension of your home for entertaining during the warm summer months. The fashion for alfresco dining has meant that these areas can be used as a delightful setting for Mediterranean-style meals as well as general relaxation. The choice of colours and fabrics for outdoor furnishings may be inspired by a number of factors, for example the amount of light received and the direction of the sun. A terrace or patio that

Left *Cushions or covers can be taken outside and used with garden furniture to provide comfort for impromptu alfresco dining.*

Making a square scatter cushion

Measure the cushion pad to be covered from seam to seam. Placing any pattern on the fabric to its best advantage, cut out two panels of fabric for the cushion cover to the size of the cushion pad, plus a 1.5cm (⅝in) seam allowance on three sides and 2.5cm (1in) extra on the opening edge.

On both panels of fabric press 2.5cm (1in) to the wrong side, along what will be the opening edge of the cushion cover. Pin the panels together along this pressed line and stitch along the line for just 4cm (1½in) at each end. Insert a zip in this opening (see page 70).

Pin the pieces together, right sides facing. Open up the zip halfway and stitch around the remaining three sides, 1.5cm (⅝in) in from the raw edges. Snip across each corner to within 6mm (¼in) of the stitching line. Neaten the raw edges and turn the cushion cover the right side out. Push out the corners using the tip of a pair of scissors. Press and insert the cushion pad.

benefits from a great deal of sunlight would suit cool Californian blues and greens, while a shadier aspect could be brightened up by using such stunning colours as brilliant oranges, reds and pinks.

Choosing fabrics

Washable fabrics are obviously most suitable for outdoor seating since covers that are out in all weathers are more likely to need regular cleaning. Check how light-resistant the fabric is, as some weaves and prints are more suitable than others. Generally, curtain fabrics and deck chair canvases will wear well. Plasticized fabrics are useful out of doors, as the PVC coating helps to prevent any colour fading and makes for an easy-care, wipe-clean surface.

Quilted fabrics provide an instant soft touch for cushions, but prequilted fabrics often have only a dress-weight top layer, which may not be as fade-resistant or durable as other heavier fabrics. Cushions and mattresses should always have

Above *Colourful cushions can complement the hues of flowering pots and containers, while making wooden furniture more comfortable.*

washable polyester fillings, so that it does not matter if they are left out in the garden overnight and caught in the rain by mistake.

New covers and linings for outdoor furniture and accessories can be made for both old and new pieces. The

Above *Conservatories and garden rooms can form a distinctive link between an indoor living space and the outside. Here, wicker furniture and soft furnishings in floral-patterned chintz mix with exotic-looking plants and outside-style flooring.*

Left *Give old sofas and chairs a new lease of life in a garden room by draping them with fabric or ready-made throws. Here, white cotton fabric with a simple printed design is accentuated by brick red cushions.*

Right *The indoors and outdoors truly seem to merge in this room, with a grape vine taking centre stage. The wooden chair seat is given added comfort with cushions in beautiful fabrics that echo the colours of nature.*

wooden frames of deck chairs and director's chairs usually outlast their slings, so it can be very economical to make new covers (see pages 56–59).

Garden rooms

Conservatories and garden rooms can be decorated with furnishings to create a further area for living and entertaining inside the house, and to remind you of outdoor life throughout the whole year, even during the winter.

Such rooms in your home form a distinctive link between an indoor living space and the outside garden, terrace or patio. You can carry the same colour scheme through from other rooms or from the hallway in the house, or use a darker or lighter tone of a colour already used. Using colours such as china blue, white and primrose yellow for the decor and furnishings adds a lovely, natural freshness and lightness to a garden room. Equally effective are other colour combinations such as apple green and white, terracottas and golds, or neutral creams and beiges, depending on the decorating style and effect that you want to achieve.

Bringing suitable garden furniture into the room helps keep the link with the garden. Blinds are ideal for a garden room as they allow maximum light into the room when raised, but necessary shade when

lowered. Be sure to line the blinds to protect the fabric from bleaching in sunlight.

Accessories can also help to enhance a garden room. They can follow a favourite theme – the obvious one is a garden

theme with lots of potted plants, botanical prints and old gardening implements on the wall. Another popular outdoor one is a seaside theme with shells, model boats and carved wooden seagulls, for example.

A LESS STRUCTURED version of the boxed seat, the soft 'bench' mattress is more of a flat pad and can be adapted to fit window seats, deck chairs and sun loungers as well as benches. It is best made in a medium-weight furnishing fabric or, for outdoor use, cotton towelling.

Buttoned bench mattress

MATERIALS

Furnishing fabric or cotton towelling for mattress and piping (see cutting instructions)

Heavyweight polyester wadding (two layers for a thin soft mattress, up to five layers for a firmer mattress), plus extra for making soft piping (see cutting instructions)

Brown paper, pencil and plate or saucer

Ready-made buttons or fabric and button forms for fabric-covered buttons (see page 71)

Button thread and upholsterer's needle

Scissors and sewing equipment

Matching sewing thread

Suitable for a sun lounger, deck chair or bench, this mattress is filled with wadding, which can be multi-layered, depending on the depth of mattress required. The fat, softly stuffed piping gives the mattress a distinctive edge; the buttoned effect can be created with standard buttons or knotted threads (see box, page 55).

MAKING THE PAPER TEMPLATE

Using the brown paper and pencil, trace around the shape of the seat for which the soft mattress is being made. Add 1.5cm (⅝in) all round for a seam allowance and then cut out the paper template. Using a plate or saucer as a guide, round off the edges to create a curved edge on all four corners for the piping. To calculate the fabric needed, multiply these measurements by two, and then add an extra 1m (1yd) for self-piping.

CUTTING OUT

Cut one top and one bottom mattress piece from the fabric, using the paper template. Cut

the layers of wadding using the paper template, and then trim 2.5cm (1in) all around to ensure that it fits inside the finished mattress cover. For fat, stuffed self-piping, measure the length of all four edges of the mattress, add 3cm (1¼in) seam allowance and cut a piece of fabric the length of this total and 15cm (6in) wide. The fabric for the piping should be cut on the bias (diagonally) and it will be necessary to join a number of fabric sections together to create the correct piping length (see page 67).

MAKING THE SOFT PIPING

Cut the wadding for the piping into 15cm (6in) wide strips. The total length of the strips should match the length of the piping fabric. Roll up the strips evenly and hand stitch loosely to secure. Lay the strip of binding fabric, wrong side uppermost. Lay the wadding rolls along the length of the binding, butting ends together. Wrap the fabric around the wadding so that the raw edges match, and baste in place along the length. This line

Above *A soft mattress creates a comfortable corner in which to sit and relax in comfort.*

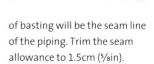

of basting will be the seam line of the piping. Trim the seam allowance to 1.5cm (⅝in).

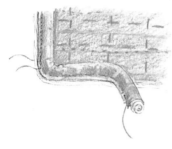

machine stitch in place along the line of basting stitches.

Lay the layers of wadding on the wrong side of the top panel fabric and baste in place with a grid of basting stitches across the mattress.

SEWING THE PIPING TO THE FABRIC

Lay the piping along the right side of the fabric designated for the top panel of the mattress, with its raw edges lying flush with the raw edge of the mattress piece. Baste the piping around the top panel edges then

JOINING THE MATTRESS SECTIONS

With right sides facing, baste the top and bottom mattress panels together. Stitch them together along the same stitching line as the piping, leaving an opening of approximately 20cm (8in) in one short edge. Press the seams, turning back and pressing the

seam allowances along the opening at the same time. Clip and notch the seam allowance around the corners as illustrated and turn the mattress fabric to the right side. Slipstitch the opening closed.

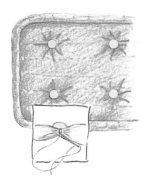

SEWING ON THE BUTTONS

Mark out the positions of the buttons evenly on the top panel of the mattress, using crossed pins or tailor's chalk. An average mattress would require eight buttons – four down each side. Stitch the buttons on firmly through all layers of fabric and wadding, using button thread and an upholsterer's needle. Unpick the grid of basting stitches. If necessary, stitch ribbon ties at the corners of the mattress so that it can be tied to the seat frame.

Optional finishes

- Instead of using buttons to finish the mattress, take six strands of embroidery thread and stitch through all the layers of the mattress from top to bottom and through to the top again. Repeat to make a second stitch in the same place. Knot the ends together and trim carefully, leaving tails of about 5cm (2in) on each end. Repeat for a fuller effect.

- For a tailored effect on the mattress, use standard piping cord and 2.5cm (1in) wide bias-cut strips in place of the soft piping.

Left *A boxed wooden garden bench provides a focal point in a sunny garden room. A long boxed seat cushion is combined with a soft bench mattress for a back cushion and side 'pillows', held to the frame with fabric ties.*

Right *A soft, comfortable mattress in a pretty checked print softens the harsh lines of an old metal-framed chair.*

Deck chairs and director's chairs

WORN OR SHABBY-LOOKING director's chairs or deck chairs can be given a new lease of life with easy-to-make covers, or slings as they are often called. Narrow-width deck chair fabric is available in many different patterns and colours, and its ready-finished selvage eliminates the need for making any seams. However, it is possible to use other fabrics of similar strength and in different patterns and colourways, which can be cut and seamed to fit.

Making a new cover for a deck chair from deck chair fabric actually requires no sewing at all, since the fabric is folded under at both ends, slung from the wooden deck chair frame and secured with rows of upholstery pins. Slings and covers for director's chairs do generally require sewing, but they are very simple to make. A small pillow is easy to make and adds a little luxury to a basic deck chair.

Above right *A headrest in the form of a small padded pillow in matching fabric gives this deck chair a little extra touch of comfort. Floppy decorative bows add a feminine touch.*

Right *A classic deck chair with a worn seat can be given a new look with a cotton striped cover.*

Making a deck chair sling and pillow

TOOLS AND MATERIALS

Deck chair fabric or heavyweight canvas for cover and head pillow – standard deck chair fabric is available in a 46cm (18in) width (see cutting instructions)

Hammer and upholstery pins

Scissors and sewing equipment

Matching sewing thread

Feather or foam filling for pillow

Stick and sew touch-and-close fastening

MEASURING AND CUTTING OUT
To calculate the length of fabric required, fold the deck chair completely flat and measure its length from the front lower edge of the fixing bar, around the bar, down to the lower bar and around the lower bar to the front upper edge. Add about 20cm (8in) to this to allow for folding the fabric under the frame, and a further 63.5 cm (25in) of fabric for the pillow. Cut out the fabric pieces.

ATTACHING THE FABRIC TO THE UPPER FIXING BAR
Turn under 10cm (4in) at both ends of the fabric. Position one folded edge level with the front lower edge of the upper fixing bar and tack it in place by hammering upholstery pins through the folded fabric into the underside of the fixing bar.

ATTACHING THE FABRIC TO THE LOWER FIXING BAR
Pass the fabric over the bar and down the length of the chair. Check the folded edge will wrap under the lower fixing bar and fit tightly, then open the chair out and tack upholstery pins along the lower edge as before.

MAKING THE PILLOW
Take the 63.5 cm (25in) of fabric for the pillow and cut it into two pieces, one 50cm (20in) long, the other 12.5cm (5in) long. Fold the 50cm (20in) length of fabric in half, right sides facing, and stitch along both side seams and for 2.5cm (1in) at each end of the opening. Turn the fabric the right side out, pushing the corners out using the tip of a pair of scissors. Press the raw edges along the opening to the inside of the cover. Insert the filling. Cut the final 12.5cm (5in) piece of fabric to the pillow width. Turn under a 1cm (3/8in) double hem along two short edges and one long edge. Attach the 'sew' half of the touch-and-close fastening to the long hemmed edge, insert the raw edge into the opening in the pillow cover and topstitch to close. Attach the 'stick' half of the touch-and-close fastening to the upper fixing bar of the deck chair and attach the pillow to the chair.

Making a director's chair cover

TOOLS AND MATERIALS

Deck chair fabric or heavyweight canvas for cover (see cutting instructions)

Scissors and sewing equipment

Matching sewing thread

Hammer and upholstery pins

Above *Director's chairs can be re-covered in a fabric of your choice and the wooden frame painted to suit.*

Director's chairs have higher backs and are more obviously chair-like than deck chairs. They can therefore be useful indoors as well as outside, unlike deck chairs which tend to be kept mainly for use on the beach or in the garden.

Some director's chairs need to be taken apart before a new cover is fitted; others require panels of fabric with purpose-made 'sleeves' stitched at each side to be fitted over the bars of the frame. The instructions that follow are for attaching panels of fabric to the chair frame using upholstery pins.

CUTTING OUT

For a standard wooden director's chair you will need to cut out a piece of suitable fabric measuring 65 × 40cm (25½ × 16in) for the chair seat and another piece 65 × 20cm (25½ × 8in) for the back of the chair.

NEATENING THE EDGES

Make a turning of 1.5cm (⅝in) along the longer edges of each piece (i.e. the front and back edges of the chair seat and the top and bottom edges of the chair back). Machine stitch the hems in place.

ATTACHING THE SEAT FABRIC TO THE CHAIR FRAME

Turn under 5cm (2in) along the shorter edge of each fabric panel. Take the fabric for the chair seat and align one folded

Below *Director's chairs are useful outdoors or for occasional indoor seating and can be folded away for neat storage.*

edge along the underside of the side seat fixing bar. Tack upholstery pins along the fold to hold the fabric in place. Wrap the fabric over the top of the bar, across the frame, over the second fixing bar and around to the underside. Tack the second folded edge firmly in place with upholstery pins.

ATTACHING THE CHAIR BACK FABRIC TO THE FRAME

Repeat the process to fix the fabric for the chair back around the side fixing bar in the same way, to finish the chair.

Picnic rugs

A RUG WILL BRIGHTEN up any summer expedition when you are having a picnic out in the open, and saves you from having to sit directly on the ground, be it in grassy countryside or on a sandy beach. A rug with a practical PVC backing is even better and means that it can be used on damp ground. Although you can buy ready-made picnic rugs, if you make your own you can make it to coordinate with picnic accessories such as tablecloth and napkins – or even the lining of your picnic hamper – for stylish alfresco eating.

PVC-backed picnic rug with carrying strap

MEASUREMENTS

Size of rug: 150 × 150cm (60 × 60in), rolling up to a bundle about 38cm (15in) long with a 100cm (40in) carrying strap

MATERIALS

Fabric for rug (see above) – 1.5m (1¾ yd) of 150cm (60in) wide heavyweight fabric

Waterproof backing fabric – 3.2m (3½yd) of 90cm (36in) wide fabric

Scissors and sewing equipment

Cotton or nylon webbing for carrying strap – 2.3m (2½yd) of 2.5cm (1in) wide webbing

10cm (4in) of 2.5cm (1in) wide touch-and-close fastening

Matching sewing thread

This picnic rug rolls up neatly so you can carry it with a custom-made strap. The strap is secured around the rug with touch-and-close fastening, but buttons or buckles would do instead. For the fabric for the rug use plaid or tartan check wool, blanketing or heavy-weave cotton fabric such as waffle-weave cotton. You could even use a ready-made rug if you remove the fringe around it. For the backing fabric, use water-resistant cotton, PVC or thin nylon fabric.

CUTTING OUT THE FABRIC

Trim the main fabric to a square, 150 × 150cm (60 × 60in). Cut the backing fabric in half and join the two side edges together with a flat fell seam (see page 65). Trim the backing fabric to the same size as the main fabric.

BACKING THE RUG

With right sides together, stitch the rug to the backing fabric all around the edges, taking a 1.5cm (⅝in) seam. Leave an opening along one edge, about 25cm (10in) long. Trim the seam allowances and clip the corners.

Turn the fabric the right side out, pushing out the corners using the tip of a pair of scissors, and press the edges. Along the open edge, turn under and press the seam allowance and baste. Topstitch around the edge of the backed rug, approximately 1cm (⅜in) from the outer edge. Fold the rug in half with the woollen side inwards, then fold it again along its length. Roll up the rug and tie with two pieces of string to check how long the webbing straps need to be.

CUTTING THE WEBBING

Having checked the quantity of webbing required in the previous step, cut two lengths of webbing for the straps to go around the rolled rug – these will probably need to be about 55cm (22in) in order to go around the

rug, with an overlap of 5cm (2in) and a turning allowance of 2.5cm (1in) at each end. Use the remaining webbing for the main carrying strap – it should be about 105cm (41in) long.

SEWING THE FASTENING TO THE STRAPS

Halve the length of touch-and-close fastening. Peel open each short strip of touch-and-close fastening into two separate pieces. Take the two shorter lengths of webbing and turn under 2.5cm (1in) to the wrong side at one end of each. Position a piece of the touch-and-close fastening over each of these turnings then topstitch in place. At the other end of these straps, turn the webbing to the right side and stitch the remaining strips of touch-and-close fastening in place.

MAKING THE CARRYING STRAP

Turn under 2.5cm (1in) at each end of the long webbing length for the carrying strap. Stitch one folded end of this strap to the centre of each of the shorter straps, with the wrong face of the carrying strap against the right faces of the other straps.

Top *The bright checks of this colourful picnic rug, backed with a waterproof PVC lining, are ideal for a summer picnic lunch.*

Above *A simple carrying strap makes transporting the rug extremely easy.*

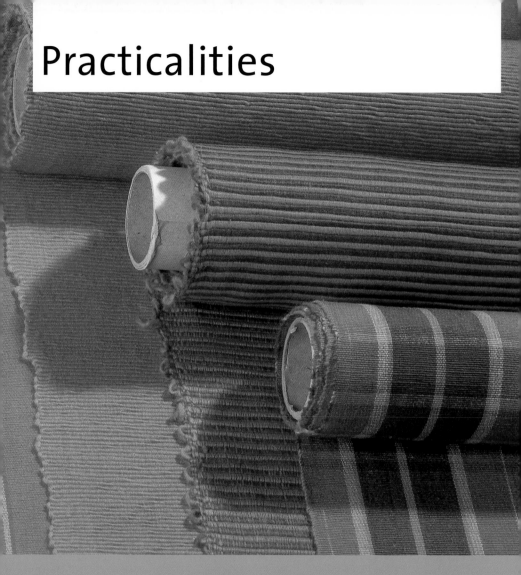

Practicalities

TO ENSURE THE SUCCESS of your soft furnishing projects, it is worth learning some sewing techniques that will give your seating covers and cushions a professional finish. The following pages cover basics such as cutting fabric and matching patterns, stitching seams and hems, adding fastenings and knowing how to use interlining. More decorative matters include covering buttons, plus learning how to make piping and frills. These can be fitted into almost any flat seam and look very effective, yet neither is difficult to make. Piping is particularly useful for defining the shapes of seams to give loose covers and cushions a stylish finish, while frills give furnishings an attractive edge.

Cutting fabric and using patterns

WHATEVER TYPE of project you embark upon, you will need to cut out panels of fabric – usually cut on the straight grain for making up loose covers and square cushions, or cut to shape for irregularly shaped chair cushions.

The first stage in a sewing project is marking out cutting lines and other features accurately, and then cutting the fabric. Lay the fabric out flat before starting, and ensure that it remains flat as you cut it. When cutting rectangular panels, you will get a much better finish with good-quality fabric with a straight weave.

Never use the selvage as the edge of a panel of fabric when sewing: the selvage may be tightly woven, preventing the fabric from falling naturally, and the unprinted selvage area may not be the width of the seam allowance required.

Pattern pieces

For some projects you may want to mark a pattern shape directly on the fabric, using tailor's chalk. Alternatively, use a paper pattern as a cutting guide – brown parcel paper is good as it does not tear easily. If you are making a set of tie-on cushions, for example, you can ensure all the pieces are the same if you draw the shape on brown paper, cut out the paper pattern, then pin the pattern on the fabric so that you can cut around it. When cutting a pattern piece, make a note of whether or not you have included a seam allowance. It is sometimes easier to add the

seam allowance when you cut out, by cutting 1.5cm (⅝in) away from the edge of the paper pattern. To cut several layers of fabric at once, pin them together to prevent them slipping (which would distort the shape of the fabric pieces).

PATTERN MATCHING

When joining panels of patterned fabric, you need to match the pattern along seam lines, particularly with bold patterns on throws or loose covers. Allow a slight margin of error when cutting out the fabric, then join the widths of fabric, as follows.

Press under the seam allowance of one fabric piece, then position it on the second piece so that you can see the right side of both pieces to be joined. Move the folded edge over the other piece until the pattern matches. Pin the seam allowances together from beneath the fabric.

Pressing and ironing

Pressing is an integral part of good sewing. While ironing helps remove wrinkles and creases, pressing is a more precise technique: working on a small area at a time, you use the heat and steam from an iron to flatten details, lifting the iron up and down. Use the point of the iron to get into corners.

Pressing your seams as you work will give you much better sewing results. After stitching a straight seam, press along the line of stitching to set the stitches into the fabric, then open out the seam and press the seam allowance open from the wrong side. Pressing is particularly important for items such as loose covers and cushion covers, which need turning the right side out once stitched.

Seams

MOST SEWING involves seams – long straight seams down throws, for example, and bulky piped seams in cushions and upholstery. Some seams are decorative, while others need to be invisible. For strength, most seams are stitched by machine, but in some cases you may prefer to sew by hand, using a fine running stitch or backstitch.

Before machine stitching a seam, match the edges to be joined carefully, with right sides facing, and pin the layers together close to the stitching line. Position your pins at right angles to the stitching lines, so that the points just reach the seam line. If you prefer, baste the layers together before stitching the seam.

Flat seams

A flat seam is commonly used for joining fabric widths. To make a seam lie flat and prevent unsightly lumps on the right side of the fabric, you may need to trim and layer the seam allowance, particularly if there are several layers of fabric. If this is the case, trim each layer a different amount, so that the edges do not all fall together when the seam is pressed. Also trim, notch and clip the seam allowances of curved seams and at corners, so that when the piece is turned the right side out, you will have a smooth unpuckered curve or a crisp corner. You can also neaten the edges of a seam allowance by trimming it with pinking shears, with a zigzag or overlock stitch, by turning under and stitching the raw edges or, with a heavy fabric, you may prefer to bind the raw edges with bias binding.

STITCHING A FLAT SEAM

Stitch the seam with the right sides facing and raw edges matching. Normally, a 1.5cm (⅝in) seam allowance is used. Reinforce the ends of the seam line by reverse stitching.

LAYERING SEAM ALLOWANCES

Trim each seam allowance in a seam by a different amount to reduce bulk. This technique is particularly important for a smooth fit on items with bulky, piped seams, such as loose covers for armchairs and sofas.

CLIPPING CORNERS

On a corner, such as that on a cushion or loose cover, clip away the seam allowance diagonally across the corner. For particularly bulky and sharply angled corners, you can taper the seam allowances further, to reduce the thickness of the fabric in the corner when the cover is turned the right side out.

CLIPPING AND NOTCHING CURVED SEAMS

On an outer curve, for example on a circular cushion cover, cut little notches out of the seam allowances every 2.5–5cm (1–2in) so that when the cover is turned the right side out the fabric lies flat. Similarly, on inner curves, clip into the seam allowance, so that when the item is the right side out the edges of the seam allowance lie flat.

STITCHING CORNERS

When stitching around corners in particularly bulky fabrics, such as when making heavyweight loose covers, it may be difficult to create a neat corner. A couple of extra stitches, diagonally across the corner, will allow for the fabric's bulk.

Stitch to just before the corner's point, stopping with the needle in the fabric. Lift the presser foot and pivot the fabric 45° around the needle. Lower the foot and make two stitches diagonally across the corner, stopping again with the needle in the fabric. Lift the foot, pivot again, then continue stitching the seam.

Flat fell seam

A flat fell, or run-and-fell, seam is a flat seam that encloses the fabric's raw edges without creating too much of a ridge in the fabric along the seam line. The seam is highlighted with a line of stitching running down beside it. On the back of the seam, you can see two parallel lines of stitching.

A flat fell seam is useful for joining seams that will be under strain, such as a lined picnic rug and for seams that may be seen from either side – on a reversible throw, for example.

STITCHING A FLAT FELL SEAM

Stitch a normal seam, with right sides of the fabric facing and raw edges matching. Press the seam, press it open, then press both seam allowances to one side. Trim the seam allowance pressed closest to the fabric to 1cm (3/8in) then turn under 6mm (1/4in) along the uppermost seam allowance. Pin and baste the upper seam allowance to the fabric, enclosing the raw edges of the lower seam allowance. Topstitch the length of the seam close to the folded edge.

Hems

THE EDGES OF MOST soft furnishings have to be carefully finished to ensure that they look good and do not fray when laundered. The options are to hem the edge or to bind it with a matching or contrasting fabric.

Hems are generally intended to provide an almost invisible finish to the edge of an item. The traditional dressmaker's hem involves a narrow turning, and then a deeper turning, which can be adjusted at the final fitting stage. Most hems or edges in home sewing, however, are double hems, with two equal turnings, to give a crisper finish. Hems can be stitched in place by hand for an invisible finish, by machine using a special hemming stitch (see below) or they can be topstitched by machine.

Mitring hems

One problem area with hems lies in getting a neat finish at corners on square items. To finish corners neatly, the hems have to be folded to create a diagonal pleat – a procedure known as mitring. At the same time, excess fabric is trimmed away so that the corners lie flat and are not lumpy.

TRIMMING THE FABRIC
Unfold the pressed fabric. Trim the fabric diagonally across the corner, cutting 3mm (⅛in) out from the point where the fold lines cross. Press under a 3mm (⅛in) turning across the corner.

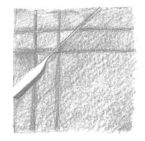

FOLDING THE MITRE
Refold the first turning of the hem, keeping the diagonal turning in place. Turn under the second fold of the hem and the edges of the diagonal turning should meet neatly at the corner. Baste in place then machine or hand stitch.

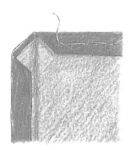

PRESSING A HEM TO BE MITRED
Where the hem goes around a corner, whether stitching the hem by hand or machine, you need to reduce the fabric's bulk by mitring for a neat finish. First press the turning allowance and the hem all round the edge of the item. This will ensure that the material is flat and the mitring cut can be accurate.

Hemstitch
Hemstitch alternates three straight stitches with a zigzag stitch, which just catches a couple of threads of the main fabric. Press the hem in place, then fold back the fabric where the hem's fold is to be stitched to the main part of the work. Stitch along the folded hemline, catching a couple of threads of fabric as the machine needle swings to the side.

Piping and frills

STRAIGHT SEAMS and hems should usually be as invisible as possible in many soft furnishings. However, you can make a feature of seams with piping and frills, outlining an item to emphasize its shape. Even if a pattern does not provide instructions for including piping or frills and flounces, they can be fitted into almost any flat seam. Bold piping or generous flounces set into seams can make a real style statement. Piping is ideal for outlining the shape of a cushion or sofa cover, while frills of gathered fabric can be used to give a soft finish to seat covers.

Making piping

Piping requires strips of fabric cut on the bias, known as bias strips or bias binding. To cover piping cord, you will need 4–5cm (1½–2in) wide strips, depending on the fabric weight and the size of the piping cord to be covered. This provides for a 1.5cm (⅝in) seam allowance, plus fabric to wrap around the cord.

Piping cord is usually made of cotton and should be preshrunk (or wash it before use) if you are inserting it in an item that is washable.

binding at right angles to this first line, then mark in the bias strips parallel to the first line. Cut out along the marked lines to give a number of strips.

JOINING BIAS STRIPS
Position two strips, right sides together, at right angles, their raw edges meeting. Overlap the pieces so that the corners extend on either side and you can stitch a seam line running from edge to edge and 1cm (⅜in) from the raw edges. Press the stitching, then press the seam open and trim away the corners. Wrap the bias strips around the piping cord, then stitch as close as possible to the cord, through both fabric layers.

MARKING AND CUTTING BIAS STRIPS
Take a rectangle of fabric and mark a diagonal, at a 45° angle to the selvage, from one corner across to the opposite edge. Measure the width of the

STITCHING PIPING IN PLACE
Position the covered piping on the right side of one piece of fabric, so that the piping stitching line matches the fabric's seam line and the raw edge of the piping covering is towards the raw edge of the fabric. Stitch in place, using a piping foot on the sewing machine (see page 68), adjusted so that the needle is between the foot and the piping cord. Position the second panel of fabric on top of the piping, right side facing inwards, and stitch again along the same seam.

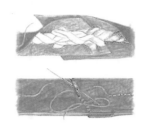

TURNING CORNERS

Where the piping goes around a corner, stitch in place as far as the corner, then snip into the seam allowance of the piping covering at the corner point, so that you can turn it around the corner. If the corner is gently curved, make several cuts into the seam allowance so that you can ease it into position.

JOINING ENDS OF PIPING

After pinning piping in place, cut the ends of fabric diagonally (following the fabric grain) and cut off the piping cord, leaving a 1.5cm (⅝in) seam allowance at each end. Unravel the piping cord at the overlap and entwine the loose ends together. Turn under the binding seam allowances and slipstitch together.

RUCHED, OR GATHERED, PIPING

This gives a sumptuous finish to seams. Use the heaviest piping cord you can find. Cut the fabric for binding the piping on the straight grain or the bias; its width should be at least eight times the diameter of the cord. Cut the cord and binding to 1½ times the finished length of the seam to be piped. Wrap the binding around the cord and baste in place. Stitch 3–6mm (⅛–¼in) from the cord. Stitch across one end of the piping, through the cord and binding to secure it. Slide the binding down the cord. When sufficiently gathered, stitch across the open end of the binding to hold the cord in place, and trim away the extra cord.

Stitching a zip or piping

Use the narrow zip/piping sewing machine foot to stitch near a zip's teeth. The foot can be adjusted to stitch on each side. The narrow foot is also used to stitch binding closely in place around piping cord or to stitch the covered cord to fabric in a seam.

Frills and flounces

Frills of matching or contrasting fabric can be inserted into seams, for example around the edge of a tie-on seat cushion or a scatter cushion, or topstitched to fabric, for example around the bottom edge of a loose cover. For an inserted frill, a folded strip of fabric is usually used, which saves hemming; a topstitched frill needs its raw edges finished before you gather and stitch the frill. Decide how wide you want the frill before cutting the fabric.

PREPARING THE FRILL

Cut a strip of fabric that is equal in width to twice the width of

the finished frill, plus seam allowances. The frill length should be 1½–2 times the length of the finished seam. Neaten the ends of the frill by folding the strip in half lengthways, right sides facing. Stitch the short seams at each end, press, trim the seam allowances and turn the right side out. Push out the corners neatly using the tip of a pair of scissors then press the frill strip.

GATHERING THE FRILL

Gather the frill with machine or running stitch. If you are using running stitch, make two rows of stitches, quite close to each other, staggering the positions of the stitches to prevent pleats from forming. Draw up the gathers until the gathered frill length matches the length of the seam where it is to be stitched. Anchor the gathering threads around a pin at each end of the frill. Check that the fullness is evenly distributed along the frill and pin or baste it in place on the fabric panel.

SETTING IN THE FRILL

Begin by stitching the frill to the right side of one of the fabric panels, with raw edges matching, making sure that the fullness is distributed evenly. Position the second fabric layer (for example the back of a cushion cover) right side inwards, over the frill and stitch the seam. Press, trim the seam allowances and turn the fabric to the right side. Allow extra fullness at corners if the frill extends around the corner.

PIPED AND FRILLED FINISH

For extra detail, combine piping with a frill in a seam. Position the piping along the raw edge of the top panel, and stitch in place. Then position the gathered frill and stitch. Finally, position the back panel of fabric, so that the piping and frill are sandwiched in place. Stitch the seam. Trim all seam allowances, press and turn the fabric to the right side.

TOPSTITCHED FRILL

Cut the fabric for the frill to the width of the desired finished frill, plus a turning allowance. The length of the fabric strip should be 1½–2 times the gathered length of the frill. Turn under the hems all round and stitch, using a fine zigzag stitch or make a double hem. Gather the frill along the stitching line as before, then topstitch it in place on the fabric panel, distributing the fullness evenly.

Holding fast

MANY SOFT FURNISHINGS, for example loose covers and cushions, need openings so that they can be easily removed for cleaning. These openings need fastenings to keep them closed while in use. Fastening by the length (touch-and-close, hook-and-eye or press-stud tape) is often used for loose covers, but zips are much more often used for cushion covers. Touch-and-close fastenings are useful on some heavy-duty items, while hooks and eyes, press studs and buttons are often more economical. Closures are often fitted in the seam lines of cushions and loose covers, but it can be easier to set them across a panel of fabric – especially where piping or frills are involved – to give seams a neatly piped outline. Home-made fabric ties (see page 44) are another closure option for cushions and loose covers.

Fastening by the length

Nylon touch-and-close fastening comes in long strips made up of a double layer: one half has tiny hooks and the other has a soft mesh of nylon loops. When joining two fabric pieces, allow an overlap equal to the width of the fastening you are using. Also allow for turning under each of the edges to be joined. Topstitch the fastening to the wrong side of the overlap and the right side of the underlap. Fix lightly with glue before stitching them, as the backing is very difficult to pin in place. Use the mesh of loops on the overlap and the crisper hooks on the underlap.

Position hook-and-eye and press-stud tapes in the seam allowance or along an overlap. The eyes of the hook-and-eye tape, and the sockets of the press-stud tape, should be on the right side of the underlap; the hooks and the studs should be on the underside of the overlap. Topstitch in place. Do not stitch close to the metal or plastic inserts in the tapes.

Hand-sewn fastenings

Individual hooks and eyes, and press studs are sewn on by hand; and buttons are best sewn by hand for a secure finish. Mark the position of these closures carefully, and check both halves are aligned accurately before stitching in place.

Stitch hooks and eyes on with several stitches around the link of each. On an overlapped closure, the hardware should not show when the fastening is closed. The eye or bar should be on the underlap.

Align the two halves of a press stud by pushing a needle through the central hole, and through both fabric layers to be joined. Stitch the stud on the overlap and the socket on the underlap.

Setting a zip in a cushion panel

Set a zip between two flat panels, close to the seam line to be less intrusive. On boxed cushions, set the zip into a side panel before making up the cushion.

JOINING THE PANELS

Decide where the zip should be in the panel. Make a paper pattern of the panel's finished dimensions and cut it along the zip line. Use the two patterns to cut out the fabric, adding 2.5cm (1in) seam allowances along the edges where the zip will be. Baste the two pieces together along the position of the zip, taking care to match patterned fabric, if appropriate. Stitch a little at each end of the seam

line, leaving unstitched the part where the zip will be. Leave the seam basted along the zip line.

POSITIONING THE ZIP

Press the seam, then press the seam allowances open (including along the basted section). Position the zip behind the seam, so that it is centred over the basted seam line. Pin and baste in place, then, working from the right side, topstitch the zip in place, across the ends and down both sides.

Use a zip or piping foot (see page 68) to avoid damaging the zip. Do not stitch close to the zip or the fabric will gape and the zip will be difficult to operate.

Buttonholes and loops

Buttonholes can be stitched by machine (see your sewing machine manual for detailed instructions). Rather more elaborate to make are rouleau button loops (see page 44), created by stitching a long fabric tube into loops down the overlapping edge of a closure. These can be spaced apart on the soft furnishing item or butted together for a more dramatic effect. The loops have to be set into a seam down the opening edge of the item, created by a facing of fabric.

ATTACHING ROULEAU LOOPS

Set the rouleau loops into a faced opening, so that the raw loop ends are enclosed. Position the loops next to each other for a traditional 'buttoned dress' finish, or space them apart down the opening for less work! Pin the loops along the raw edge on the right side of the overlap, with raw edges matching. Stitch

in place, then position the facing over the loops, right side down, and stitch the seam. Press, turn the facing to the inside and press again.

Fabric-covered buttons

Covered buttons look very effective with rouleau loops – small buttons for tightly spaced loops, and larger buttons for a more casual effect. They are also good for studding a bench mattress or cushion (see page 55).

Cover buttons with fabric to match the cover you are making, or add plain-covered buttons to a patterned item. For extra detail, coordinate the buttons with the rouleau loops.

Button forms are available from haberdashery departments in a range of sizes, complete with instructions. If you are using very fine or slippery fabric, use iron-on interfacing to give the fabric a firmer finish before covering the button.

COVERING A BUTTON

Simply cut a circle of fabric a little larger than the diameter of the button (you will find precise

instructions with the button form) and tuck it over the front portion of the button before fixing the button back in place.

Interlinings

THERE ARE MANY WAYS you can improve a finished project by adding extra hidden layers as you make up the item. Interlinings are soft fabrics that give extra body to soft furnishings. Traditional interlinings include bump and domette; other types include flannelette and synthetic wadding (available with iron-on backing for quilted projects). Check that your chosen interlining will wash (or dry clean) with the fabric with which it is being used.

Using interlining

Interlining is a bulky fabric, so join widths of it by machine with lapped seams or by hand using herringbone stitch to prevent any stiffness at the join. Once the item is made up, the interlining is enclosed by the main fabric and lining, so its raw edges are protected from fraying.

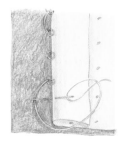

LOCKING IN INTERLINING

To prevent interlining slipping around inside between layers of fabric, for example if you are making a throw (see page 38), lock it to the wrong side of the main fabric before making up the throw. Lockstitch is a long, looped stitch, worked down the length of the fabric on a fold in the interlining. Pick up only a single thread of the main fabric and do not pull the thread taut.

JOINING INTERLINING OR WADDING

To join layers of wadding or interlining with minimal bulk, use a wide or multi-zigzag stitch. Overlap the seam allowances, machine stitch with zigzag stitch and then trim away the excess fabric.

For bulky layers of wadding or very thick interlining, butt together the edges that are to be joined, and stitch by hand with herringbone stitch (see box below), taking stitches across the join on alternate sides.

Herringbone stitch

Herringbone stitch is decorative as well as being useful for a firm hem where you want a minimal bulk, for example, with very thick fabrics. Do not make an extra fold in the hem – simply neaten the fabric's raw edge with zigzag stitch before making a herringbone-stitch hem.

Working from left to right, bring the needle up through the hem, then insert it in the main fabric diagonally up to the right. Take a tiny stitch in the main fabric, then move the needle down diagonally to the right and take a stitch right through the hem. Repeat this stitch all along the hem.

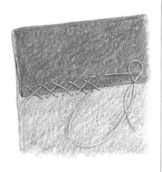

Decorative extras

THERE ARE MANY DIFFERENT BRAIDS, fringing, cords and ribbons available for adding decorative detail to soft furnishings without having to make custom-made piping and frills. Look round a haberdashery department for ideas for ready-made finishes. Some are intended for setting into seams in the fabric, others are topstitched in place before making up an item. Silky, rope-twist insertion cord, which has a flange woven into it to stitch into the seam, gives a luxurious touch to cushions and covers; woven braids can be stitched to throws and loose covers and glued to upholstered chairs, while fringing can emphasize seat edges.

Finishes for seams and hems

Flanged insertion cord is used to emphasize seam lines in the same way as covered piping cord. Position it along the seam line of the main panel of fabric, and stitch it in place using a piping foot (see page 68), taking care to stitch only the flange and not the cord itself. Stitch the second panel of fabric on top to complete the seam.

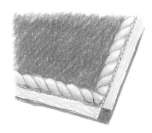

USING INSERTION CORD

Stitch the flanged cord in place to the right side of one panel of fabric, just as for stitching piping in place (see page 67), before completing the seam.

COPING WITH CORNERS

If the insertion cord has to fit around a curve or corner, first clip into the flange so you can then more easily manoeuvre the cord into place.

Topstitched finishes

When applying a topstitched finish, such as braid, fringing or ribbon, mark its intended position on the fabric, using tailor's chalk. The decoration should be applied before making up an item such as a cushion cover. This makes it easier to work with and, where the trimming runs to the item's edge, you can be sure the raw edges will be stitched into the seam as you make up the item.

TOPSTITCHING

Pin and baste the trimming in place, then topstitch it by machine. Wide trimmings should be topstitched close to each edge with straight stitching, or use a narrow zigzag stitch worked over the trimming's edge. If you are making two lines of stitching, work them both in the same direction to avoid twisting and distorting the trimming. Very

narrow trimmings can be held in place with just a single line of straight or zigzag stitching along the trimming's centre.

Facts and figures

CHOOSE TO WORK in either imperial or metric, but do not mix the measurements. For quick reference, a series of conversion charts is given below: detailed conversions of small amounts, fabric yardage/metrage and common fabric widths. These last two charts are for use in stores that sell by the metre when you have worked out quantities in yards.

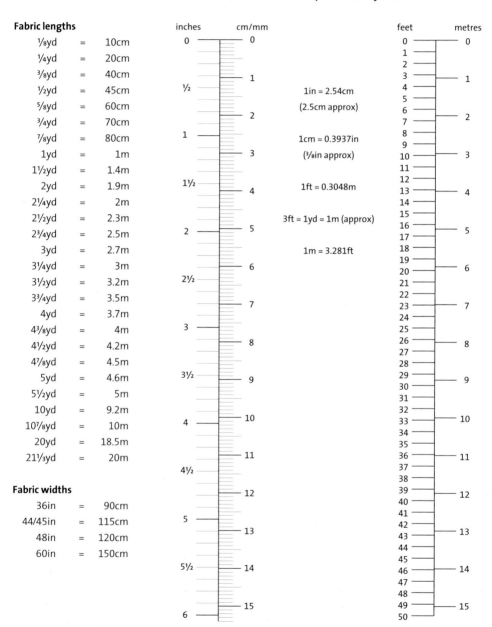

Fabric lengths

⅛yd	=	10cm
¼yd	=	20cm
⅜yd	=	40cm
½yd	=	45cm
⅝yd	=	60cm
¾yd	=	70cm
⅞yd	=	80cm
1yd	=	1m
1½yd	=	1.4m
2yd	=	1.9m
2¼yd	=	2m
2½yd	=	2.3m
2¾yd	=	2.5m
3yd	=	2.7m
3¼yd	=	3m
3½yd	=	3.2m
3¾yd	=	3.5m
4yd	=	3.7m
4⅜yd	=	4m
4½yd	=	4.2m
4⅞yd	=	4.5m
5yd	=	4.6m
5½yd	=	5m
10yd	=	9.2m
10⅞yd	=	10m
20yd	=	18.5m
21⅓yd	=	20m

Fabric widths

36in	=	90cm
44/45in	=	115cm
48in	=	120cm
60in	=	150cm

inches cm/mm

1in = 2.54cm
(2.5cm approx)

1cm = 0.3937in
(⅜in approx)

1ft = 0.3048m

3ft = 1yd = 1m (approx)

1m = 3.281ft

feet metres

Glossary

Acrylic Synthetic fibre used to make fabric that has similar properties to wool.

Appliqué Method of decorating fabric by stitching on shapes cut from other fabrics.

Basket weave Woven effect in fabric with several strands of warp and weft threads running together to create a small block effect.

Binding (bias and straight cut) Narrow fabric strips used to cover the edge of a larger panel of fabric; bias binding is cut diagonally across the fabric (on the bias) so that it can be eased around curves without pleats or puckers.

Bound button holes Tailored buttonholes finished with strips of fabric binding, rather than machine- or hand-sewn buttonhole stitch.

Braid Woven trimming, used for topstitched decorations on cushion covers and other soft furnishings; braids are more substantial, and often more elaborately woven, than ribbons.

Brocade Medium- to heavyweight fabric, woven in two colours to make a satin background with a relief pattern.

Broderie anglaise Cotton fabric that has been pierced and embroidered for a decorative effect; available as a full-width fabric or as a narrow trim; usually white or cream.

Bump Thick fabric, traditionally a loosely woven brushed cotton, that is used both to improve the wear of curtains and give other furnishings a soft and luxurious feel.

Button loops Fabric or hand-stitched loops that act as buttonholes. Fabric button loops are also known as rouleau loops.

Calico Medium-weight cotton cloth, usually white or unbleached; its low price makes it suitable for making cushion pads filled with foam or polyester stuffing.

Canvas Heavyweight cotton fabric, often used for deck chair covers.

Casing A channel in a piece of fabric made by folding over the top and doing two lines of stitching; used to make fastenings for loose covers, draw-string bags, etc.

Check A grid pattern, usually woven but may be printed on to fabric.

Chenille Subtly ribbed, velvety fabric, softer in texture than velvet or corduroy.

Chintz From a Hindu word, chintz is a printed cotton fabric, usually glazed (glossy), but the term is now used to denote any glazed cotton fabric.

Clip To cut into fabric at right angles to the raw edge, or diagonally across corners, in order to prevent any possible distortion of curved seams and bulk in corners when an item is turned the right side out.

Complementary colours Colours that lie on opposite sides of the colour wheel: the pairs are red and green; blue and orange; yellow and purple.

Corduroy Heavyweight fabric with pile woven into the fabric to form narrow ribs.

Covered buttons Buttons covered with fabric; they can be made with special button forms, available from haberdashery departments and stores.

Crewel work Flowing style of embroidery, developed in 16th-century Europe, usually in wool on linen.

Damask Fabric (usually silk or linen) with a pattern woven into it; often woven in a single colour, so that the pattern only shows as the light catches the fabric.

Denim Originally from the city of Nîmes in France, a twill weave fabric traditionally woven using indigo warp and white weft threads.

Dobby weave Fabric woven with small, repeating pattern, like a diamond or raised star.

Domette Soft fabric, often synthetic, used as a layer of padding in soft furnishings.

Dressmaker's carbon paper Paper with coloured coating on the back, so that when you trace an outline on it, the motif is transferred to a layer of fabric beneath the carbon paper.

Drop-in chair seat An upholstered panel that can be lifted out of (or dropped into) the frame of an upright chair.

Duck Originally used for sails and outerwear, this plain weave fabric in cotton or linen is hard-wearing, and can be used for making loose covers.

Easy-care fabrics Usually woven from a mix of fibres, and requiring minimal ironing.

Electronic sewing machine Electric sewing machine with microchips to make it easy to adjust the type, size and tension of the stitch.

Facing Panel of fabric used to back the main fabric of a cushion or other item around the opening, for a neat finish.

Field The background colour of printed or embroidered fabric.

Flat seam A simple seam used to join two pieces of fabric with a single line of stitching.

French seam Double seam in which the raw edges are completely enclosed.

Geometric print Regular print, of abstract shapes arranged in a regular pattern.

Gingham Lightweight woven fabric, usually white and one other colour, originally a striped fabric, but now used to describe check.

Grain of fabric The lengthways grain is the direction in which the warp threads of the fabric run, parallel to the selvages.

Ground The 'background' fabric used in appliqué, embroidery, etc.

Gusset A narrow panel, sometimes shaped or gathered to give fullness; the side panels of a box-shaped cushion.

Herringbone A fine, hand-sewn stitch, used to join panels of wadding or to hold hems in place;

may also be used as an embroidery stitch.

Ikat Fabric woven from predyed yarn; the yarn is coloured in sections so that predyed patches are woven in next to each other to create a pattern.

Interfacing Layer of fabric, often synthetic, non-woven and iron-on, used to stiffen light-weight fabrics and make them easier to handle. In soft furnishings it may be used to stiffen fabrics used for appliqué motifs.

Interlining Soft fabric (usually domette or bump) used to add weight and luxury to some soft furnishings.

Jacquard Fabric with colour-woven pattern, similar to brocade or damask; named after the inventor of the loom on which it is woven.

Lapped seam Seam made by overlapping the edges of the panels of fabric to be joined.

Lawn Fine plain-weave cotton fabric.

Layer To trim the seam allowances within a

seam to different lengths, eliminating bulk.

Linen union Plain weave fabric made from a mixture of linen and cotton threads.

Lining Layer of fabric added to give improved wear.

Liséré Embroidered and beribboned or elaborately woven fabrics and trimmings.

Lycra Brand name for a stretch fibre (elastane).

Matelasse Padded cushion or mattress.

Mercerized cotton thread Sewing thread specially treated to improve wear and look more lustrous.

Monochromatic scheme Colour scheme that uses only one colour (plus white) in varying tones.

Monotones Scheme using only one tone of a colour.

Motif Abstract or figura-tive outline or pattern on printed or woven fabric, or pattern used for embroidery, appliqué, etc.

Muslin Fine, loosely woven cotton fabric, commonly available in white or natural.

Notch To cut a V-shaped wedge out of the seam allowance; this is done so that pieces of fabric can be matched when they are being stitched together, and also to reduce bulk in curved seams when an item is turned the right side out.

Organdie Fine stiff cotton, open-weave fabric, now often available in synthetic fibres.

Organza Finely woven stiff silk, made from a particular type of twisted silk yarn.

Ottoman Heavy, twill-weave fabric, in silk, linen, cotton or synthetic fibre.

Overlock machine Advanced sewing machine that forms stitches in a more elaborate way than a traditional sewing machine; particularly useful for stretch fabric.

Over-stuffed seat Upright chair or stool with upholstery that extends right over the top of the seat and a short way down the chair frame.

Paisley An intricate pattern with elongated and curved oval motifs, originating in India but taking its name from the Scottish town renowned for its textile industry.

Petersham ribbon Hard-wearing, ribbed ribbon, traditionally made of silk.

Pile The 'fur' of a carpet or of a velvety fabric.

Pincers Scissor-like tool used in upholstery to lift old nailheads and tacks.

Piqué Light- or medium-weight cotton fabric woven in a single colour with a fine, embossed effect.

Plaid Colour-woven fabric (a check).

Polyester wadding Thick, soft, lightweight padding available in standard widths and thicknesses.

Primary colours The three basic colours – red, blue and yellow – from which all other colours can be mixed (with the addition of black and white).

Provençal print A small, geometric interpretation of paisley patterns, printed in strong colours on lightweight plain-weave cotton.

Pucker Unsightly gathering along a seam line, caused by a blunt needle or a bulky seam.

PVC A plastic coating applied to fabrics to make them waterproof and wipeable.

Rayon A synthetic fibre – the first one to be developed – that imitates silk.

Rouleau A fine tube of fabric, often used as a fastening.

Ruching Gathering fabric to create a panel of luxurious folds.

Sateen Cotton fabric woven to produce a glossy effect.

Satin A type of weave in which warp threads run over the surface of the fabric to give a glossy finish; a silk fabric with a satin weave.

Satin stitch Closely worked stitch; may be worked in lines by sewing machine or over larger areas by hand.

Scrim Stiff, loosely woven lightweight linen fabric.

Seam allowance The allowance around the edge of a piece of fabric for making a seam. Always add a seam allowance to the finished dimensions before cutting out fabric.

Seam line The marked or imaginary line around the edge of a piece of fabric marking the line of stitching when a seam is made.

Seam tape Firmly woven narrow cotton tape that is used to prevent seams from distorting; the seam tape is positioned along the seam line on the wrong side of the fabric, and stitched into the seam when the layers of fabric are joined.

Secondary colours The three colours – purple, green and orange – obtained by mixing any two of the primary colours.

Seersucker Plain woven fabric, often striped or checked, in which groups of warp and/or weft threads are drawn tighter, creating rows of ruching down or across the fabric.

Selvage The woven, non-fraying edges of a length of fabric.

Serging machine See overlock machine.

Shot silk Silk fabric woven with different colours for the warp and weft, creating a fabric that reflects different shades as it catches the light.

Silk dupion Fabric made from silk spun by a particular type of silk-worm: two silkworms spin a double cocoon producing a double thread that can be unravelled for weaving.

Squab Small cushion tied to the seat of an upright chair.

Taffeta Plain fabric, usually silk, with a glossy, stiff finish.

Take-up lever Lever on sewing machine that moves up and down to allow the thread to loop through the fabric as you stitch.

Tartan Originating in Scotland, tartan is wool fabric woven to create a checked design; each clan or family tradition-ally had its own particular tartan.

Template A pattern; when cutting repeated identical shapes, for appliqué or patchwork, the template is cut out in card so that it can be used over and over again.

Tertiary colours Colours containing all of the three primary colours.

Thread count The number of threads in a specified area (a square inch) of a woven fabric.

Ticking Tightly woven fabric with a distinctive woven stripe; tradition-ally featherproof with black and off-white stripes, but now avail-able in a range of natural and muted colours.

Toile de Jouy Cotton fabric, originating in 18th-century France, with figurative scenes printed in a single colour on a neutral background.

Topstitching A bold line of stitches used to emphasize seams or finish hems.

Touch-and-close fastening Synthetic fastening, made with tiny plastic loops on one half, which link into a furry mesh of nylon hoops stitched to the opposite side of the opening.

Towelling Woven fabric with a looped pile on both sides.

Trim To cut away excess fabric.

Twill (weave) A weave in which the warp threads form a diagonal rib over the surface of the cloth.

Velvet Woven fabric with a pile; may be made from a wide range of fibres.

Warp The threads that run up and down a woven piece of cloth.

Webbing A broad woven braid. Traditional hessian webbing or modern rubber webbing is used in upholstery; webbing from synthetic fibres or cotton may be used for straps and ties.

Weft The threads running across a woven piece of cloth.

Welt A name given to the gusset or side panel of a boxed cushion.

Wild silk Silk fabric made from natural silk fibre, but not from the *Bombyx mori* (mulberry silkworm) native to China.

Yarn Thread (natural or man-made fibre) that has been spun or twisted so that it can be woven or used for embroidery or knitting.

Index

Acknowledgements

Photography

Crown Paints back cover bottom left, 2, 10, 29 bottom, 47 bottom

Elizabeth Whiting Associates 4 bottom, 23, 41, 56 top

Anna French Ltd 9 top, 12, 51

Octopus Publishing Group Ltd.

    Rupert Horrox 16, 40, 47 top, 50 bottom, 56 bottom, 58, 61 top, 61 bottom

    Sandra Lane 7 top

    Di Lewis 3, 25, 26, 39 bottom

    Peter Myers 27 bottom, 39 top

    David Parmitter front cover top, back cover centre left, back cover top left, 1 top, 4 top, 14, 19, 21, 34, 37, 38, 42, 44, 44 bottom, 45 top left, 45 top right

    Paul Ryan 1 bottom, 32, 33

    John Sims 7 bottom

    Debi Treloar 5 top, 8, 11, 13, 15, 62

    Steve Wooster 50 top

    Polly Wreford 5 bottom, 6, 29 top, 46, 48, 49, 55

The Interior Archive/Fritz von der Schulenburg front cover bottom, 30, 59

Lelievre 53

Liberty Furnishings 9 bottom

Sanderson 18, 22, 27 top, 28, 54

For Hamlyn

Editorial Manager: Jane Birch
Senior Designer: Claire Harvey
Project Manager: Jo Lethaby
Designer: Mark Stevens
Picture Researcher: Christine Junemann
Senior Production Controller: Louise Hall
Illustrator: Jane Hughes